Novelist, playwright, critic and campaigner, BRIGID
BROPHY, F.R.S.L., was born in mid-1929 in London,
where she lives. She was trained successively as a
shorthand-typist and as a classical scholar at Oxford, from
which she was sent down. She is married to Sir Michael
Levey, the novelist and art-historian who in January 1987
retired early from the directorship of the National Gallery.
They have a daughter and a grandson. Since 1984 Brigid
Brophy has been progressively crippled and invalided by
multiple sclerosis.

READS

Brigid Brophy

Cardinal

SPHERE BOOKS LTD

Published by the Penguin Group
27 Wrights Lane, London, w8 5TZ, England
Viking Penguin Inc., 40 West 23rd Street, New York, New York 10010, USA
Penguin Books Australia Ltd, Ringwood, Victoria, Australia
Penguin Books Canada Ltd, 2801 John Street, Markham, Ontario, Canada, L3R 1B4
Penguin Books (NZ) Ltd, 182–190 Wairau Road, Auckland 10, New Zealand

Penguin Books Ltd, Registered Offices: Harmondsworth, Middlesex, England

This collection first published in Great Britain by Sphere Books Ltd 1989

Printed and bound in Great Britain by
Richard Clay Ltd, Bungay, Suffolk

Contents

The Menace of Nature

So? Are you just back? Or are you, perhaps, staying on there for the extra week? By 'there' I mean, of course, one of the few spots left where the machine has not yet gained the upper hand; some place as yet unstrangled by motorways and unfouled by concrete mixers; a place where the human spirit can still – but for how much longer? – steep itself in natural beauty and recuperate after the nervous tension, the sheer stress, of modern living.

Well (I assume you're *enough* recuperated to stand this information?): I think you've been piously subscribing to a heresy. It's a heresy I incline offhand to trace, with an almost personally piqued sense of vendetta, to the old heresiarch himself, the sometimes very great, often bathetic, but never cogently thoughtful poet, William Wordsworth. Since the day he let the seeds of heresy fall (on, no doubt, the Braes of the Yarrow or the Banks of Nith), the thing has spread and enlarged itself into one of the great parroted, meaningless (but slightly paranoid) untruths of our age.

I am not trying to abolish the countryside. (I *state* this because it is true; I emphasize it because I don't want the lynch mob outside my window.) I'm not so egoistical as to want the country built on or littered up with bottles and plastic bags merely because it doesn't appeal to *me*. The country is the best conceivable home for wild mammals and birds – or it would be if humans, the only animal predators who can, if they choose, desist from predation without damage to themselves, did not wantonly attack their fellow animals.

My own taste for the countryside, though small and often wounded by human atrocities on those they misname

3

the beasts, is existent. I've found the country very pleasant to be driven through in a tolerably fast car by someone whose driving I trust and whose company I like. But I admit that landscape as such bores me – to the extent that I have noticed myself in picture galleries automatically pausing to look at 'Landscape with Ruins' or 'Bandits in a Landscape' but walking straight past the pure landscapes at a speed which is obviously trying to simulate the effect of being driven past in a car.

I'm not, however, out to dissuade *you* from spending your holiday as a sort of legalized bandit in the landscape. Neither am I anti-holiday. Holidays have been sniped at as things everyone feels an obligation to enjoy but no one really does. Yet I suspect there would be fewer dissatisfied holiday-makers if social pressure didn't try to limit our choice to 'Landscape' or 'Landscape with Seascape'. You can be made to feel quite guiltily anti-social in the summer months if you are, like me, constitutionally unable either to relax or to take a suntan. Indeed, relaxation is becoming the social *sine qua non* of the end of the century, like bridge in the 1930s. Society will scarcely let you have a *baby* now if you can't satisfy it beforehand you're adept at relaxing. Yet on the in some ways more private question of taking a holiday, constitutional urbanites are still free, if only they can resist being shamed on to the beaches, to opt out of a rest and settle for the change which even the proverb allows to be as good as it. By simply exchanging their own for a foreign city, they are released from the routine of earning their daily bread and washing up after it, but don't suffer the disorientation, the uncorseted discomfort, which overtakes an urbanite cast up on a beach with no timetable to live by except the tides.

Still, it isn't in the holidays but during the rest of the year that the great rural heresy does its damage. How many, for example, of the parents who bring up their children in London do so with unease or even apology, with a feeling that they are selfishly depriving the children of some 'natural heritage' and sullying their childhood with urban impurities? Some parents even let guilt drive

4

them out to the suburbs or further, where they believe they cancel the egocentricity of their own need or desire for the town by undergoing the martyrdom of commuting. This parental masochism may secure the child a rural heritage (though parents should enquire, before moving, whether their child has the rural temperament and *wants* the rural heritage) but it deprives the parent of the cultural one; he gains the tennis club but is condemned to the tennis club light-opera society's amateur production of *No, No, Nanette* because the trains don't run late enough to bring him home after the ENO.

The notion that 'nature' and 'nature study' are somehow 'nice' for children, regardless of the children's own temperament, is a sentimental piety – and often a hypocritical one, like the piety which thinks Sunday School nice for *them* though we don't go to church ourselves. Historically, it is not inept to trace the supposed affinity between children and 'nature' to Wordsworth's time. It was about then that there settled on Britain, like a drizzle, the belief that sex is *not* 'nice' for children. Children's sexual curiosity was diverted to 'the birds and the bees' and gooseberry bushes; and birds, bees and bushes – in other words, 'nature' – have remained 'suitable' for children ever since.

If the romantic belief in children's innocence is now exploded, its numinous energy has only gone to strengthen the even more absurd romantic belief in the innocence of landscape's, as opposed to man-created, beauty. But I reject utterly the imputation that a brook is purer than Bach or a breeze more innocent than *As You Like It*. I shall be suspicious of this aesthetic faculty of yours that renders you so susceptible to the beauty of Snowdon if it leaves you unable to see anything in All Souls', Langham Place; and I shall be downright sceptical of it if (I am making allowance for your sensibility to run exclusively in that landscape groove which mine leaves out) you doat on the Constable country but feel it vaguely impure to take a bus to the National Gallery to see a Constable.

You'll protest you feel no such impurity. Yet didn't you

5

read the first paragraph of this article without taking so much as a raised eyebrow's worth of exception? Didn't you let the assumption pass that the city is corrupt? Weren't you prepared to accept from me, as you have from a hundred august authorities – sociologists, physicians, psychologists – that *idée reçue* about the nervous tension and stress of modern urban life? But what in heaven's name is this stressful modern urban life being compared with? Life in a medieval hamlet? Will no one take into account the symptoms into which the stress of *that* erupted – the epidemics of dancing madness and flagellation frenzy?

The truth is that the city is a device for *reducing* stress – by giving humans a freer choice of escapes from the pressure (along with the weather) of their environment. The device doesn't always work perfectly: traffic jams *are* annoying; the motor car does maim and must be prevented from doing so; but the ambulance which arrives so mercifully quickly is also powered by a motor. The city is one of the great indispensable devices of civilization (itself only a device for centralizing beauty and transmitting it as a heritage).

It is one of the cardinal simple brilliant inventions, like currency. Like currency, it is a medium of exchange and thereby of choice – whereas the country is a place where one is under the thumb of chance, constrained to love one's neighbour not out of philanthropy but because there's no other company.

What's more, in the eighteenth century the city was suddenly upgraded from a device of civilization to a manifestation of it. The city became an art form. (The form had been discovered, but not very widely remarked, earlier. It was discovered, like many art forms, by accident – often, as at Venice and Bruges, an accident of water.) We are in dire danger now of clogging up our cities as devices and at the same time despoiling them as works of art; and one of the biggest villains in the process is our rural heresy.

Most western European beings have to live in cities, and all but the tiny portion of them who are temperamental rustics would do so contentedly, without wasting energy in guilt, and with an appreciative eye for the architecturescapes round them, had they not been told that liking the country is purer and more spiritual. Our cities run to squalor and our machines run amok because our citizens' minds are not on the job of mastering the machines and using them to make the cities efficient and beautiful. Their eyes are blind to the Chirico-esque handsomeness of the M1, because their hearts are set on a rustic Never-Never Land.

Rustic sentimentality makes us build our suburban villas to mimic cottages, and then pebble-dash their outside walls in pious memory of the holiday we spent sitting agonized on the shingle. The lovely terraced façades of London are being undermined, as by subsidence, by our yearning, our sickly nostalgia, for a communal country childhood that never existed.

We neglect our towns for a fantasy of going 'back' to the land, back to our 'natural' state. But there isn't and never was a natural man. We are a species that doesn't occur wild. No pattern in his genes instructs man on what pattern to build his nest. Instead, if he's fortunate, the Muses whisper to him the ground-plan of an architectural folly. Even in his cave, he frescoed the walls.

All that is infallibly natural to our species is to make things that are artificial. We are *homo artifex*, *homo faber*, *homo Fabergé*. Yet we are so ignorant of our own human nature that our cities are falling into disrepair and all we worry about is their encroachment on 'nature'.

For, as I said at the start, the rural fantasy is paranoid. A glance at history shews that it is human organization which is frail, and civilization which flickers in constant danger of being blown out. But the rural fantasy insists that every plant is a delicate plant. The true paranoid situation is on the other foot. I wouldn't wish to do either, but were I forced either to pull down a Nash terrace or to build over a meadow, I'd choose the latter. If you don't like what you've put up on the meadow, you can take it away again and the meadow will re-seed itself in a year or two; but human semen is lucky if it engenders an architectural genius a century. The whole Wordsworthian fallacy consists of gravely underestimating the toughness of plants. In fact, no sooner does civilization admit a crack – no sooner does a temple of Apollo lapse into disuse – than a weed forces its wiry stem through the crack and urges the blocks of stone further apart. In London during the Second World War, the bomber engines were scarcely out of earshot before weeds leapt up on the bombed site. (My mother called them loosestrife, a name that seemed apt to plants apparently set loose by the strife of war, but more accurate botanists have told me they were more probably rosebay willowherb.) Whether we demolish our cities in another war or just let them tumble into decay, the seeds of the vegetable kingdom are waiting to seize on the rubble and sprout through the cracks. *Aux armes, citoyens*. To your trowels and mortar. Man the concrete mixers. The deep, mindless silence of the countryside is massing in the Green Belt, ready to move in.

*Simenon, Novelist, and
Maigret, Novelist*

The Train, whose French text appeared in 1961 and of which Hamish Hamilton issued the translation into English by Robert Baldick in 1964, is probably the novel his admirers had been expecting all along from Simenon. If we aren't satisfied now, we are ingrates.

It had been a problem of, precisely, satisfaction. Despite the fame and the high-class praise, Simenon's reputation has never quite been established *enough*, and I think it's because before *The Train* no one book has ever clicked quite satisfactorily home. He was a master – an acknowledged master – without (quite) a masterpiece. Virtuoso technician, he was eluded by some tiny technical knack. Novel after novel was without fault; something much less important, some mere and hardly more than mechanical flaw, disrupted their proportions. This is nothing, of course, to do with the absolute size. *The Train* has the usual Simenon brevity. He simply gives more condensed value than the standard package.

In the puzzle or suspense novels, the disproportion is inherent in the genre. Anticlimax is inevitable when the resolution of a book includes the solution of a mystery or the sudden dispersal of terror. Stories in that form are always a little less than legitimate – they really do deceive. When you sit down with them, they present magnificent, athletic torsos: only when it's time to rise do you discover that their legs are withered away. With Simenon the maiming is all the more conspicuous because the torso is *so* fine. The dénouement shews him up as the victim of his own genius for building suspense to Colossus size. But even in his most 'straight' novels there is, if less noticeably, a topheaviness. Probably it comes from the resolute defeatism, the low relief, of his vision. Since this is implicit in the very manner of his writing from the start, it makes for an overloading of the first third of the book: a little too much of the conclusion is already stated in the major premise. The conclusion therefore doesn't carry quite the right weight, doesn't make quite the decisive home-coming click of surprise plus inevitability. To work, as Simenon determinedly does, with a muted – a rainy – palette invites the same difficulties about the moment of home-coming as singing in a minor key. Simenon is too versed a craftsman to go sour on the key note, but one senses his having to feel round for it; he comes to it, finally, with not quite enough breath.

In *The Train* he achieves perfect breath control. So far as I can scrutinize it, the miracle (artistically it's nothing else) is worked by almost literally invoking heaven. Simenon always composes on two planes (perhaps the ultimate disproportion in the other novels is a flawed gear-change between them): he incarnates the universal in the particular. Like Chardin, he creates an artistic archaeology – people are implied by their possessions and their utensils; and his method, like Chardin's, is to *super*-saturate these objects in their own essence, so that something spills over into universality.

And when you come to his people – come on them, as it were, *in* their things – they in their turn are *so* particularized, just as his settings are *so* localized, as to become general. I think the psychology of it must be that he makes the habits and idiosyncrasies of his characters so known to the reader that each and every reader emotionally equates the character with the person of his most intimate acquaintance, himself. Similarly, localities realized in such exact and penetrating detail can be treated by the reader's emotions only as the one locality we have all apprehended in truly vivid detail, the setting of our childhood.

The Train is built up by this method: but also, in counterpoint, by its opposite. Simenon's favourite theme, a personal moral failure, is set against a whole nation's failure of morale. The time is the early summer of 1940 – as he establishes by a single observation of period clothes: a woman on the train is 'wearing a blue serge skirt, which was too tight and riding up her hips, and a white blouse marked with rings of sweat, through which you could see her brassière'. You always could see the brassière through 1940 blouses. The train itself is taking refugees from near the Belgian border deeper into France, but it hardly outstrips the German armies. Marcel, the first-person narrator, decides to abandon his radio repair shop and his hens (all over Europe, wartime must be evoked by the importance taken on by hens) and, with his wife and small daughter, join the train. On it, his family rate better accommodation than he does; he is separated from them, and presently their carriage is shunted off. Marcel goes on, in the overcrowded cattle-truck, to – it turns out – La Rochelle. In transit and at the reception centre at La Rochelle he has, with a fellow-refugee, one of the most poignant love affairs in twentieth-century literature.

As always in Simenon, the love is foredoomed. Myopic, ex-tubercular, Marcel has never expected to achieve a 'normal' life – a metaphor, in terms of the external, real political world, for the sense we all have of inward handicap; no sensitive person has ever expected to achieve a normal life. Marcel cannot rise to the occasion of his love affair and transcend his marriage – because the marriage itself seems higher than he could have aspired. It is implied all through that he conscientiously will pursue his inquiries through the disorganized channels of bureaucracy, discover where his wife has been taken and return to normality, which he knows will mean abandoning, and half knows will eventually mean betraying, his mistress. But Simenon has for once opened this closed world, this inevitably open-and-shut case, to the sky. Not only does the puddle reflect the heavens; the heavens are invoked to reflect the puddle. Simenon has done nothing so pretentious as to write an allegory of the fall of France. He has used that as, in the jeweller's sense, a setting: he sets the feeling of wartime extraordinariness against the extraordinariness, the sense of a détour taken out of normal time, of a love affair. The much-played-on irony that France fell in a brilliant summer is in Simenon's hands doubled back on itself. The blue sky of national disaster is the blue sky of happiness, of childhood recovered, for his hero. Simenon, who has evoked so many moods by means of weather, now employs the pathetic fallacy at its most biting. The perfect sky which rains machine-gun bullets is also the sky of a pastoral idyll.

Simultaneously with *The Train* the same publisher issued Jean Stewart's translation of an exceptionally good Maigret, *Maigret et son Mort*. I have long held that the Maigret books let us into Simenon's workshop, Maigret himself being essentially a novelist. Eternally dispossessed, eternally a Belgian in Paris, the novelist sits on the Métro wondering about the man opposite: what does such a man carry in his pockets, what sort of room does he go home to at night? If Maigret is a detective, it's because only the detective – once the victim has been opportunely knifed – has the chance to search the room and itemize the contents of the pockets. Maigret's relationships are almost always more with the victims than with the assassins. He doesn't really want to know whodunit – only what it was like to be the victim before it was done. Other detectives demonstrate the triumph of ratiocinative, Maigret of imaginative reconstruction. They sit and think; he sits and imagines. He has a novelist's passivity. (One of the few blunders in the workmanlike transposition of Maigret to television was that in one episode Maigret drove a car. The real Maigret can't drive. He is, to his marrow, a passenger.) *Maigret's Special Murder* is a refined example of the novelist-detective method. Maigret is tantalized by having spoken to the victim on the phone and by having *almost* caught sight of him from that window on the Quai des Orfèvres, before he becomes a corpse reconstructible from its effects. When he does, the corpse becomes Maigret's property: 'Alors, Maigret, et "votre mort"?'

The book also adds to our knowledge of Maigret's ineradicable lower-middle-classness. Here, as in so many of his cases, Maigret is contrasted with the well-born and *au-*

fait judge Coméliau, who is in charge of the *instruction*. Maigret's social standing probably represents Simenon's own Belgianness, a motif Simenon cannot leave alone even in French settings: this time, the former proprietor of a Parisian *brasserie* ('of the sort Maigret liked, not yet modernized') announces himself as a Belgian and adds 'I'm not ashamed of it, you know!' It is in this book that we learn that Maigret addresses his wife, on the phone, as 'madame Maigret'. The translation can't give the full incongruity, since he combines the formality with *tutoyer*ing her: 'C'est toi, madame Maigret?' She addresses him as 'Maigret'. But in a story (included in the volume *Maigret et l'Inspecteur Malgracieux*) written eight years later Simenon added an apparently post-dated explanation of the habit: 'Depuis toujours, peut-être parce qu'une fois ils l'avaient fait en riant, ils s'appelaient Maigret et Mme Maigret.' Not until (in *Maigret chez le Coroner*) he goes to the United States do people ask Maigret point-blank what his first name is. Then (since 'il ne pouvait pourtant pas leur dire qu'il n'en avait pas') he admits to 'Jules'.

Not until *Les Mémoires de Maigret* did he recount the conspiracy against him when he was a young, *pudique* and easily blushing inspector of the Police des Mœurs: his colleagues at the Quai des Orfèvres did not know his first name but the prostitutes of Paris contrived to find out; as he patrolled his (and their) beat, one after another would murmur from doorways as he passed: 'Bonsoir, Jules!'

A Literary Person's Guide to Opera

A forlorn title, that, for who would confess to being literary?

It is one of the neglected puzzles of comparative aesthetics that the word 'literary' is everyone's outcast. Unlike its counterparts, 'literary' isn't wanted even on home ground. Whereas it is a compliment to call a musician 'musicianly' or a painter 'painterly', you do not call a writer 'literary' – still less 'bookish' – unless you mean to insult him. Yet 'literary' won't transplant, either. A writer is glad to be told that his sentences are melodious, and a painter that his colours – or an architect that his proportions – achieve harmony. But none of the arts aspires to the condition of literature. Let some not very talented Victorian paint a picture which tells a story, and his work is condemned as 'literary'. But let Rubens paint the 'Judgment of Paris' or Tiepolo paint 'Sophonisba receiving the Poison', and connoisseurs give those Old Master-pieces the more dignified name of history or mythology pictures, though in point of fact they tell a story every bit as much as 'And when did you last see your father?'

It seems to me that the position of the literary element in opera is analogous – tolerably strictly – to its position in 'history pictures'. And of course the first point on which the analogy rests is that in both cases the literary element is very, very subordinate indeed. An opera whose music is bad can no more be saved by a superb libretto than the superb story about Paris and the three goddesses can save a painting of it if the painting happens to be by a bad painter instead of Rubens. No one in his senses would claim that the literary part of an opera can stand alone, shore up the music or even make an equal contribution to the total. I want only to urge that it need not be detrimental to the music.

I expect few people would say in so many words that they think the very existence of the libretto a pity, and that it's sad that so many great composers suffered the inexplicably wayward folly of putting so much of their greatest music into operas. Yet I suspect, perhaps unjustly, that there is implicit in some operatic criticism and comment a belief that to pay serious attention to the plot and characters would somehow taint the purity of the music and impugn the critic's musical sensitivity. Puritanisms of this sort do arise in some temperaments, and sometimes get taken up and made into a fashion. When as an adolescent during the 1940s I was becoming acquainted with the orchestral repertory through the help of my (slightly) elders and musical betters, it was definitely implied to me that no person of the smallest musical acumen would ever listen to the cadenza in a concerto – especially not in a violin concerto.

If one was following the score, one usually *had* to stop at that point anyway, since the cadenza wasn't printed, but even if one was listening with one's ears alone one was meant to switch off one's attention and gaze ostentatiously round the concert hall in order to signal that one had switched off: cadenze were 'impure', virtuoso confections of the nineteenth century (even when they in fact dated from the eighteenth century or the twentieth), designed for the flashy and unmusical tastes of fashionable audiences. Not till I was quite grown-up did it occur to me that this was merely wanton puritanism. If the cadenza *was* horrible, it really would not corrupt me to listen to it for three-quarters of a minute; on the other hand, it might be a rather charming little piece, but that I would never discover if I declined to listen to it. Above all, I was not obliged to choose between the cadenza and the rest of the concerto. It was highly improbable that the cadenza would be a work of such irresistibly seductive bad taste as to put my ear out and ruin my powers of appreciation before the 'pure' and 'proper' music had time to begin again.

Yet I strongly suspect that some temperaments do actually fear a corruption of this sort if they let themselves attend to the (tainted word) 'literary' part of an opera – or, indeed, of a painting. A few decades ago it was the fashion to look at a picture such as the Rubens 'Judgment of Paris' and see both a certain composition of diagonals and pyramids and a certain sensuous contrast between the painted textures of naked human flesh, landscape and peacock, and yet deliberately to exclude from one's mind – because, not being visual, it can't in the literal sense be *seen* – the information that one of the naked women is Juno and that that is why there is a peacock in the picture.

To behave like this is certainly artificial: it is to bite back the first, childish question that comes to mind when you happen on the picture. If you happened on three naked women and a peacock in the course of a country walk instead of a visit to the National Gallery, you would certainly seek an explanation – just as the purists who make a point of not reading the libretto before sitting through *Lucia di Lammermoor* would certainly demand what was going on were they staying in a Scottish country-house-party when a girl suddenly ran downstairs in a bloodstained nightdress.

Still, to be artificial is not necessarily wrong in artistic matters, art being by definition artificial. This particular artificiality, however, seems to me mistaken because it is not necessary. It is not a case of training and concentrating the mind on the work of art by excluding anything which could distract and interfere. It is, rather, an inhibition of an irrational kind; the 'literary' element is dreaded simply through superstition; were it admitted, it would not interfere and might enhance.

Of course, if you had to opt for *either* composition and texture *or* the 'story' of the picture, you would be bound to take the former, because those are exclusive to Rubens and constitute what is masterly in the masterpiece, whereas the subject of the Judgment of Paris is shared by several quite indifferent painters. But there is no need to choose – any more than there is to choose between words and music in opera. The mind is quite sophisticated enough to take in that one and the same area of paint is *both* a splendid rendering of peacock-texture *and* the emblem of a goddess, or that one and the same sound of a certain frequency is *both* top C *and* the heroine's shriek of distress. With all respect to the debate between the composer and the poet in *Capriccio*, there really is no dispute; if it's a question of which is first in importance, the music wins hands down; and it is, of course, one's musical ear one takes to the opera house: but if the experience should offer also to delight one's literary ear (as happened in the 1960s with the revelation of Congreve's words in *Semele*), it would be the most wantonly puritanical defiance of the Life Force to slip in an ear-plug. Literary pleasure is not anti-musical but a happy bonus – as though a person one was in love with anyway turned out also to have won on a Premium Bond.

As a matter of fact there are resemblances between the sensitivity of the musical and of the literary ear which are still insufficiently explored. Most of the recent approaches have come from the musical side, made by composers seeking a song-speech idiom. But some musical poet might be able to illuminate the strange fact that vowels have inherent (though not constant) pitch. Composers have long known (and so have translators of libretti when the music is already fixed) that some vowel sounds are almost impossible for a singer to articulate comprehensibly on a high note near the top of his or her compass. In a line of verse the succession of vowel-sounds is probably akin to the melody in music; and I have noticed that when someone who (as I do) lacks the talent for reading poetry aloud tries to clinch, say, a final rhyming couplet and fails, the displeasingness of the failure is remarkably like that of trying to clinch, but just missing, the final note of a tune. I suspect, in fact, that poetry-reading can be quite literally off-key.

My own deepest conviction is that form is one and indivisible, and constant for all the arts. Andrew Marvell's perfect poem to his coy mistress divides its forty-six lines into three paragraphs. I took it first for a concerto in three movements and then for an instance of what analysts of music call 'sonata form', which is by no means confined to sonatas but may be discerned in an aria or a movement of a symphony. In the title essay of my 1987 volume *Baroque-'n'-Roll* I recognize it as an argument in the form of a syllogism. Two premises (two statements) lead to a logically inevitable conclusion.

I suspect that our appreciation of form is originally kinetic – that, at the bottom of all the layers into which our sensitivity has been educated and transported by experience, we mentally *travel* the shape of a work of art, in a way we probably learned from being carried round in the womb, before we had much acquaintance with the sensations of touch, sight or hearing. If that is correct, it would make sense to say that the sensuous content in every art is a metaphor (though never *only* a metaphor) for the underlying form; and it would not be surprising if the metaphors were rather fluid and interchangeable, so that one art could slip into – and quickly out again from – the rôle of deputizing, illuminatingly, for another.

In opera, I believe, the business of the literary element is to provide sometimes a metaphor and sometimes a perspective for the music. Its obvious rôle as a metaphor is to lend specificness to music's notoriously ambiguous descriptive powers. Virtually the only thing music can represent unambiguously is the cuckoo – and that it can't differentiate from a cuckoo-clock. Handel's music to 'As when the dove' is to my ear a very precise account of the cooing and even the curious little jerks of the head made by doves in love: but music is *par excellence* like the stain on the wallpaper which might be a Red Indian or might be a chestnut tree, and if an historian told me that *Acis and Galatea* was originally composed as a chinoiserie cantata I should no doubt hear those little jerks as a perfect description of eating with chopsticks.

The descriptive metaphor a libretto provides is always conditional; it fixes, as it were, one possible aspect of shot silk; and as if to indicate its conditional nature it is often a metaphor (or a simile) in the literary sense, a metaphor within the libretto itself. *Acis and Galatea* is not *about* doves; it's a case of '*as when* the dove' – the libretto itself is playing with, trying out, the possible images.

With the utmost brilliance and dexterity this happens in the Italian libretti written by Metastasio, whose grand fame filled eighteenth-century Europe and who is in the 1980s wickedly under-esteemed. In precocious boyhood and in adulthood Mozart set arias snipped from Metastasio texts; and his last opera – composed for Prague in the last year of his life, 1791 – *La Clemenza di Tito* (K.621), was to a text Metastasio wrote in 1734 before Mozart was born. It was, Mozart noted, made into a real opera by Caterino Mazzolà, who cut and refashioned the text to the tastes of fifty-seven years later.

Metastasio was born in Rome in 1698 and was appointed Caesarian Poet at the Vienna court in 1729. He remained Italian librettist to the emperor of Austria until his death in 1782. Mazzolà, who refashioned his *Tito* text into the words Mozart set, was for a short period one of his successors as Caesarian Poet.

In the 1988 edition, published by Libris, of my book *Mozart the Dramatist*, I have tried to pay tribute to Metastasio as well as tracing the Italian pun that named him Metastasio by translating the surname he was born to, Trapassi, into ancient Greek.

Metastasio's 'comparison arias' are, in the positively grammatical sense, extended metaphors – which give his composer the opportunity for a musical metaphor without breaking the unities of the drama. The scene may be a prison; 'when a shepherd . . .', begins Metastasio; and at once a pastoral image lightens the prison without destroying the audience's prison-illusion, and a pastoral aria has the opportunity to flower where the plot gives no excuse for it.

The perspective which literature can lend to opera is a matter of the people in the drama (and the plot and actions which flow from them). Music has an enviable immediacy of *mood* – enviable, I mean, to writers (except, perhaps, to

24

the most lyrical of lyric poets; it is significant that the word 'lyrical' itself refers to a musical instrument). As a novelist I can much more easily express every nuance of a character's misgivings, because misgivings at least have an intellectual content, even if the intellectual content is a rationalization by the character, than I can convey the simple fact that the character is sad or happy. Had I been a nineteenth-century novelist, I would blatantly have shifted this part of my job to my reader: 'the reader will more readily imagine than my pen can describe with what happiness Emily . . .', etc. But the composer, should he have the gift of song, has only to put into Emily's mouth a few bars of ravishing melody, to which the librettist need supply no intellectual content – 'I am happy' will do very well, or even just 'ho ho ho' – and he has made the audience not merely understand but share Emily's happiness.

Moreover, his moods, unlike his descriptions, are quite unambiguous. You could read a third of the way through *Anna Karenina* before you were quite sure that the mood of the book is tragic. A hero of Handel's has only to utter three notes in a major key and receive one toot in corroboration from the trumpet, and you know he's in a mood of bravura triumph.

That, however, is all you know about him. Well, no; you know whether he's a tenor or a baritone or an alto: but whether cunning, simple-minded, boastful, brave, witty, kind to children or aggressive, the music can't in itself convey. He is incomparably, overwhelming *present*; but his past isn't implied in his present. It is the continuing individuality of a person which the story contributes. Music is supreme at the moods, the emotions, which only persons can feel; but it has small means of conveying the individual personality who feels them.

This limitation it shares with painting. (*All* portraits, by the way, are 'enigmatic'.) It is significant that history painting and opera often rely on mythology or historical fact for their subjects. An eighteenth-century history painting shews personages who often much resemble those of eighteenth-century opera and are placed in similar theatrically architectural settings; their bravura or elegiac mood is made almost as unambiguously plain as in opera; but for the personage's personality and past history the spectator in both cases was expected to apply to the common, educated-people's stock of knowledge of the Bible or the classics.

I am aware how dangerous it is to make any claim for even a subordinate importance of plot and person when, for example, Verdi was able to take the musical stuff he had already made up into *Stiffelio* and re-cut and re-sew it into *Aroldo*. Or again, how can one say that 'Dove sono' is a perfect expression of one individual personality, the Countess (Rosina) Almaviva, when virtually the same tune turns up in the Coronation Mass expressing a purely religious mood and attached to no personality? But really the danger is no greater than when one identifies a descriptive passage with the waters of the Rhine. No one is denying that out of context the waters of the Rhine could very well pass for a night on a bare mountain or Don Quixote charging a windmill. Since the music can stand alone, the libretto can be dispensed with if you don't like it; so there is no good reason to refuse to try it and see if you do. The Countess's personality and past history (which is what she is singing about) are a perspective, a funnel, down which one can gaze at that ravishing musical object, 'Dove sono'. The literature in opera is like a well-contrived exhibition or like landscape gardening or architectural town-planning, two other arts, in addition to opera, at which the eighteenth century excelled: it *arranges* the vistas down which we glimpse the objects. To my mind, the funnel of time and personality down which one contemplates the Countess's aria concentrates one's gaze on the musical essence. But anyone who finds the funnel obscuring it can simply remove the funnel: 'Dove sono' will still be there, quite unharmed, afterwards.

Call Me Madame Colette

'And my dearest friend put a circlet of gold round my wrist – my favourite metal whether it comes in the shape of a bracelet, a medal or the links of a chain.' Gold (no doubt there were sound reasons in the state of the market for preferring it to diamonds) was an old girl's best friend, and her 'dearest friend' was her third husband. The occasion was Colette's seventy-fifth birthday.

The Blue Lantern is a book of, and about, Colette's old age, describing the visitors, letters and memories that came to her, arthritis-bound, in the Palais Royal, and trips which she made, by car and chair, to witness the manufacture of scent at Grasse and of wine in the Beaujolais region. I would say that this – discontinuous, non-fiction – is not the book for Colette beginners to begin on, were it not for the unanswerability of the question: 'Which is?' From the first – that is, from Claudine – she shirked developing a narrative and, whenever plausible, told her stories through a disjointed journal. From the first she made precious little distinction between fiction and autobiography. All very well to claim afterwards that Willy forced her to write in the scandalous bits of the Claudine novels (which as Livre de Poche paperbacks still appear as by 'Willy et Colette': appended to the second name is the anachronistic and incongruously respectable 'de l'Académie Goncourt'). But she was out of Willy's power – married, indeed, to someone else – and the scandal twenty years out of date when she herself brought it up again and, by pinning the name of Claudine to her purportedly straight autobiographical memories of childhood, publicly affirmed that Colette *was*, scandal and all, Claudine. There is, in fact, no single book where readers ought to begin and by which Colette must be judged. There is only the creation of a single character, variously named Claudine, Renée Néré and Colette. Perhaps all three persons are co-equally autobiographical ('I have been able', this book says, 'to tell only of what I know'). More probably, they are all equally fictitious.

The Blue Lantern takes its title (*Le Fanal Bleu*) from the reading lamp for which Colette rigged up a shade out of the blue paper she wrote on. By its light the character Colette rigged up for herself (likewise, one might say, out of the paper she wrote on) is still vigorously at all its old devices and vices. Here is the usual talk about other-than-human animals – for which all honour to her; yet there is also talk *by* non-human animals; and Colette did not give up eating non-human animal corpses. Colette is still name-dropping: Cocteau, of course, and if Cocteau, then naturally Jean Marais. (It is Marais's dog, who, asked what he is looking for, replies 'A bidet, to drink from'.) Sadly, some of the names Colette drops have themselves dropped out of circulation. What can be conjured now with Francis Carco? Only, perhaps, that he was Katherine Mansfield's lover in 1915. (Mansfield herself, incidentally, entered in her Journal in 1914, 'Colette Willy is in my thoughts tonight'.) A section about her long relationship with Marguerite Moreno gives Colette a pretext to bring up her favourite scandalous subject – and then withdraw it, as teasingly as she once flirted her naked body behind a sheet on the stage: she takes care to sound, even if she isn't, disingenuous, with her 'We were young enough ... for our friendship to develop into the sort of schoolgirl crush which young ladies at boarding-schools find so intoxicating'.

It is all – to the last, calculated *o là là* about fly buttons – professionally French. Not that that means for export. It is the English who possess national characteristics only by contradistinction from wogs and fuzziwuzzies and, now that their empire has shrunk (fewer deserts in which to dress for dinner), suffer a doubt about their national identity for lack of anything to be contradistinguished from.

The French hardly bother to *be* French if the audience is less than French. Only one of Colette's trips in this book takes her outside France, and then not outside its language. In Geneva just after the war she gluttonizes professionally over the abundant food, pointing out with shock that in Paris milk is rationed 'even for the old'; she discovers presently that even in Switzerland some foods are short – and explodes her deepest, and most French, outrage at finding there is simply no black market on which to buy them.

Yet, as a writer, Colette is against the French grain. She, rather, *has* a grain: whereas the *génie français* has, since Racine, flowed classically without one. Where the whole tendency of French literature is, magnificently or banally, to substitute an abstract for a concrete and an intellectual antithesis for a tangible gesture, Colette's prose is forever bringing you up against whorls and knots – not merely substantives, but particular, even peculiar, substantives. Page after page in the Claudine books is footnoted with explanations of words 'en patois du Fresnoy'. In *The Blue Lantern* she lists (and Roger Senhouse resourcefully translates) the varieties and nuances of needle and thread; goes into horticultural minutiae; expounds the rustic method of gathering and her own method of eating (while her friends watch 'with incredulity and circumspection') water-caltrops. The personality this implies may be fake all through. I could believe she never set foot in the countryside, that she hired someone to coach her in her Burgundian accent, got her botany out of books, could not tell tulip from turnip, cat from dog or man from woman, and ate the revolting water-caltrops solely to provoke her friends' incredulity. (The peasant grunt with which, in that film they made about her, she bites into a raw onion has always sounded to me more like pain than relish.) What is authentic is the literary power which evokes these things in more than *trompe-l'œil* – in *trompe-la-langue* and *trompe-le-nez* – actuality. Impatiently, one might ask by virtue of what, except Colette's opportunist eye for publicity, one instantly recognizes 'Pauline' as

Colette's housekeeper, or what on earth it can matter whether Colette was or wasn't lesbian. The answer is that it matters for the same reason as it does about Albertine: that one knows Pauline in the sense one knows Françoise.

Colette's perseverance in the truly Proustian creation she carried out in life as well as on blue paper measures her narcissism. Almost auto-erotically she played with her own name (she even got as far as 'Willette Collie'); and by the same symptom she revealed that her sexual ambiguity went back to an indecision about whether to identify herself with her mother or her father. She inclined first towards the father. To call herself simply by her (and his) surname, Colette, shorn of female first names, was as blatant a claim to masculinity as the shorn hair which she adopted soon after. (Claudine herself is named after her father – his first name is Claude.) Maturity and fame made Colette into 'Madame Colette' – which was, of course, what her mother was. Colette's reconciliation and identification with her mother shewed itself not only in the open mother-worship she put (sagely after her mother's death) into *Sido* (she shared with her mother the first name Sidonie) but also in her ability to incarnate herself in the disreputable mother-figures of the novels: Chéri's mistress old enough to be his mother; the grandmother who, with an acute eye to an erotic detail, grooms Gigi's body for prostitution. And the object who is cherished, groomed? Colette again. (She confesses in *The Blue Lantern* that the only flower she did not like was the narcissus. It must have come too near the bone.) Colette is Gigi, lovingly groomed to receive a stranger's money and love, just as she had been Claudine, groomed by Willy for Willy. Colette is all those admired cats – especially the one she greeted in North America as at last someone who spoke French. She is even (how imperceptive of the journalists to keep asking what *man* modelled for him) Chéri. The transposition of sex was, of course, nothing to her. (Even Gigi can be a man's name in Italian.) And as a matter of fact Colette had been in name both 'puss' and 'Chéri' since her childhood – when her mother used to call her 'Minet-Chéri'.

The appreciating eye, the pampered body: both are Colette's. If she never actually went to bed with a woman, it was probably because she could not bear another woman to be the object of sexual admiration. (Her best novel is the one where Claudine actually does; but it may be good through its truth to Colette's fantasy life rather than to her life.) Oscar Wilde, whose epigrams in so many flashes anticipate psychoanalysis, had perhaps picked out the homosexuality in narcissism when he had Lord Goring say (just before looking in a mirror) that to love oneself is the beginning of a lifelong romance. But Wilde, with his generous propensity for falling in love with others – to the point of destroying himself – could not match Colette for fidelity to that romance. In the over-circumstantially furnished nineteenth-century-baroque brothel which was Colette's imagination, Colette was the tart (seventy-five-year-old heart not of, but set on, gold), the madame and even the establishment cat. Indeed, she was even the client. *The Blue Lantern* records that it was in Marguerite Moreno's company that she first, from the box of a music hall, saw Polaire; and it is in the tone of one old roué connoisseur to another that Moreno tells Colette before the curtain rises: 'You're going to see the strangest little creature.' Colette in fact loved both actresses – and in them herself: Polaire played Claudine on the stage; years later, Moreno played Chéri's mother, when Colette played his mistress.

The Dijon museum contains a Burgundian statue – old, battered, beautiful – of St Colette. In the pantheon-without-walls of literature, where there is none of that literal-minded insistence on belief which raised such a rumpus about Colette's funeral and where myths are prized not for their supposed factual content but for their authenticity as fictions, pilgrimage will always be made to the Blue Lantern district of the Palais Royal. Secular-Saint Colette, holy fraud, pray for us.

Slim Prancing Novelist

In 1973 I published (with Macmillan in Britain and with Barnes and Noble in the USA) an extremely plump hardback book with the title *Prancing Novelist* and the explanatory sub-title 'a defence of fiction in the form of a critical biography in praise of Ronald Firbank'.

Ronald Firbank died at an hotel in Rome in May 1926 at the age of forty. A third-generation-rich Englishman, he left money for the posthumous publication of his novels in a standard edition, having himself paid during his lifetime for the publication of some of them. In adulthood he was in the habit, made necessary by the oppression of male homosexuality then exerted by British law, of spending large parts of each year in France, Italy, Spain or North Africa.

I am far from repenting my plump book whose length equals that of all Firbank's novels and his play, *The Princess Zoubaroff*, put together. Despite praise from, and his discernible influence on, several gifted novelists, Firbank's glittering, funny and tragic genius was still in the 1970s and 1980s often misunderstood or neglected. Neither was the history of prose fiction correctly known. Its beginning is sometimes said by academics to have been some seventeen centuries later than it was. Novels of sophisticated and practised form were written in ancient Greek in the second or third century AD, and at least one enjoyable and sophisticated novel was written in Japanese in the eleventh century.

I took my title *Prancing Novelist* from the title of Firbank's novel *Prancing Nigger*. Firbank was infatuated with black people and black jazz (which occasioned the title of his unfinished novel *The New Rythum*), and

37

'prancing nigger' is the verbal arabesque or dance-step by which, in the patois Firbank invented, the black wife habitually addresses her husband, Mr Mouth.

Firbank was slim and almost anorexic in his wish to remain so. His innovative literary technique was chiefly a matter of leaving things out. My fat book in his praise is necessary but I am glad in 1989 to rescue and reprint this slim article also in his praise.

The three greatest novels of the twentieth century are *The Golden Bowl* by Henry James, *A la Recherche du Temps Perdu* by Marcel Proust and *Concerning the Eccentricities of Cardinal Pirelli* by Ronald Firbank.

Two of those great novelists were certainly homosexual and one of them was probably so in psychology and spirit.

It is certain that all three writers have mauve roots. Firbank's highest praiseword is 'artificial'. Proust's land- and seascapes are, like Elstir's own, washed on with the third or fourth rinse after impressionism. James (besides inventing Madame de Mauves) was a contributor to *The Yellow Book*. Obviously, nothing is so good for the prose as the habit of assuming a pose.

Not only the styles but the mental attitudes of all three writers have been formed by the aesthete's practice of continual refinement. Both James and Proust, however, when they think of another stroke that would bring them yet closer to their precise meaning, *add* it – a method which makes, at the same time, for solidity. Only Firbank, perhaps the most ruthless, does not build up to strength but excises to it. Most elegant of dandies, he actually devours the suits he sloughs, and presents to us only his dazzling, exotic, snakeskin-tight slimness.

His sister, instead of devouring, stored. Of her cache, her discarded dresses went to the V & A, and her brother's papers were sold. However, in 1962 Duckworth published a new Firbank volume. It printed bits of the sale catalogue; two complete early Firbank pieces and extracts from others; a facsimile glimpse at the notebooks (there is another all over the dust jacket – repeated, sensibly, on the binding); various photographs, including one of Firbank at Cambridge, desperate in running shorts, and two taken, when he was eighteen or nineteen, in Madrid, full of that *fade* charm of a hideous epoch of which Madrid is still redolent, and shewing that the young aesthete had a difficulty in keeping his mouth closed – as well as, in general, a face there was no doing anything with; and the seven chapters that were all he finished of his last novel – which is a masterpiece.

Firbank was socially observant before he became so aesthetically; but when the aesthetic faculty did develop it grew straight and sharp. His novels were admiring eighteenth-century houses while it was still fashionable to despise them; and well before most art historians or connoisseurs would have dreamt of doing any such thing Firbank hung a drawing-room in *Vainglory* with the 'blotches of rose and celestial blue' of 'a sumptuous *Stations of the Cross*, by Tiepolo'. (*Vainglory* is 1915; as late as 1941 a history of painting – still in print – concluded with a handy chart of relative importance in which Tiepolo is given a slot one-third the size of Madox Brown's.)

The early Firbank pieces published or listed in the new volume confirm Firbank's triple devotion: to French ('LA PRINCESS AUX SOLEILS', autograph manuscript), to his sister (second autograph of the same piece, inscribed 'A ma sœur adorée . . .') and to flowers. Like James and Wilde, Firbank seems to have virtually made himself French. All may have felt an impetus, practical or unconscious, to escape English law and convention, but there was also an overwhelming cultural motive fixing on France above all the rest of 'abroad', however much the rest might be plundered for its exotic value. Decadence is a rearguard revolutionary movement, and it was drawn to the soil on which THE revolution – with a traumatic effect on European culture which cannot be too much insisted on – failed.

To submit to tradition in French was in itself an act of

anti-orthodoxy; in every other department Firbank was emotionally incapable of obeying the rules. He never properly distinguished the Italian from the Spanish language: in his own, his syntax is riddled; he punctuates, as he writes dialogue, by ear – a brilliantly accurate one; the notebooks shew that he spelled on the same principle, but less accurately. It is quite probable that *The New Rythum* is so spelt because Firbank supposed it *was*. In *The Flower Beneath the Foot* he proves incapable of getting even the terminology of grammar right: when the king of Pisuerga, who usually calls himself 'we', lapses into 'I', Firbank says he has spoken in the singular *tense*.

Firbank's flower-cult (nicely exemplified in the 1962 volume by an early, mild, Henry Harland-ish story where the aristocratic hero takes a job as a gardener – and a fellow gardener sits up all night with a sick orchid) is also partly French; among its ancestors are Baudelaire's *Fleurs du Mal*. But in Firbank flowers are not only particularly personal (so many of his society women own flower shops that he could hardly help it) but actually personified (in one of the flower shops the flowers, only just avoiding Maeterlinckism, talk – after the shop is shut for the night). The unpublished juvenilia shew that the personification began early: one manuscript is entitled 'THE ROSES WERE NEVER CALLED BEFORE SEVEN ...'. It also continued late: *Prancing Nigger* contains an orchid named Ronald Firbank. Perhaps the flower in *The Flower Beneath the Foot* is Ronald Firbank – or Heather Firbank: for no doubt two of Firbank's devotions fused on the point of his sister's floral name.

In *Cardinal Pirelli* Firbank achieved what James never quite did: a commanding male figure. Pirelli is Firbank's Charlus. But in the other mature novels Firbank's predilections take him in the Jamesian direction of self-identification with women. Here he achieves what Proust never quite did: women drawn from the inside. It is not difficult to guess that he was imaginatively living more and more through the personality of Heather Firbank. He even achieves what James attempted only in disguise and what

Proust manifestly failed at: lesbians drawn from inside. In *The Flower Beneath the Foot*, which also contains that most poetically suspended (in a becalmed boat) of love affairs – between Mademoiselle Blumenghast and the Countess of Tolga (Olga and Vi) – the very nuns are in love with each other ('Perhaps I'll come back later: it's less noisy in my cell.' 'Now you're here, I shall ask you, I think, to whip me.' 'Oh, no . . .')

Eroticism plays over Firbank's surfaces like sunlight on a Watteau sleeve; and because it is so evanescent, resting for so brief a space on each facet, the effect, as with Watteau, is of tragedy. (It is because *The Flower Beneath the Foot* is, like *Pirelli*, a tragedy that one dare guess the personal identity of the flower.) The Firbank technique is that of mosaic in a glittering material. The more ruthless and masterly he became, the more spaces were left deliberately unfilled by anything except his immense power of suggesting whole characters *in absentia*. The later books are discoveries of fragmentary mosaic pavements, like the discovery of a Sappho fragment in *Vainglory*.

In his interstices lies Firbank's flexibility, which in the end encompassed not only tragedy and his unparalleled wit, but farce (four lines in *The Flower Beneath the Foot* state virtually the whole of *Clochemerle*) and wisecracks which, for the combination of no meaning with double meaning, resemble only Groucho Marx's. The butterfly net Firbank dragged through exotic places captured also homely species in exile – like Mrs Montgomery, the British but *h*-dropping governess to the royal house of Pisuerga, and Mrs Bedley, who saves her the best books in the long-exhausted lending library. One evening Mrs Montgomery's mail consists of 'only a picture postcard of a field mouse in a bonnet, from her old friend Mrs Bedley'. Fortunately, Mrs Montgomery is consoled by being wooed by Dr Babcock – 'Bollinger, you naughty man'; and as they drink, it is in accents of intensest jungle-Greene that 'for a solemn moment their thoughts went out in unison to the sea-girt land of their birth – Barkers', Selfridge's, Brighton Pier, the Zoological Gardens on a Sunday afternoon'.

Firbank is by no means a nineties author left over: he is a pioneer of twentieth-century art. One has only to snatch at this conversational fragment from *Inclinations* (1916) – 'There's the Negress you called a *Gauguin*' – to recognize that by 1924 Firbank had produced, in *Prancing Nigger*, something which, in its tropically enervated vitality, simply *is* a Gauguin. Firbank's emergence from the aesthetic movement is parallel to Gauguin's from the mists of Puvis de Chavannes or Picasso's from the pretty but (like Firbank's) Maeterlinck-verging pathos of his rose and blue periods. It is all part of the characteristically twentieth-century fusion of nineties decadence with those primitive motifs from overseas which were among the last booty sent home by the empire-builders: a fusion which amazingly, and almost overnight, turned mauve into *fauve*.

Unerring, Firbank adopted for his last book the new rhythm: jazz is also one of the twentieth century's fusions of decadent with primitive. To the Negro patois he used in *Valmouth* and fully developed in *Prancing Nigger*, Firbank now adds a free fantasia on white American slang. The novel is set in New York, where Firbank had never been. So he gives it to one of his New Yorkers to confess 'Somehow I've no desire much to visit England. I seem to know what it's like', and himself goes boldly on to invent New York, spreading over it 'a sky like the darkest of cinerarias'. The Sappho fragment in *Vainglory* is out-topped by a Praxiteles Hercules ('the Herc') shipped to the new world ('Fingers five by three, phallus ten by eight; restored . . .'). The flagellant secrets of the convent have combined with the eternal Firbank roses and both open to a rather astonishing fullness of bloom when Mrs Rosemerchant reads ('with nonchalance') in her newspaper: 'New York's New Vice: Society Women Birched With Roses . . . Widow of Defunct Senator Mandarin-Dove declares For *Gloire de Dijon* While Mrs Culling Browne Says Dorothy Perkins Are Best.' And at the first climax of the novel (beyond which it hardly continues) the flower-cult bears, at last, marvellous fruit – in a strawberry-picking party in *indoor* strawberry-beds.

Some reviewers have suggested that the proper reception to accord *The New Rythum* is to be a little tired of Firbank. What *do* they (to quote a thunderflash of dialogue from the *New Rythum* notebook reproduced on the cover) mean? . . .?!

Genet and Sartre

> J'entends déjà tomber avec des chocs funèbres
> Le bois retentissant sur le pavé des cours.

Thus Baudelaire: and the *retentissement*, having reverberated down a century, was caught up and reissued by the opening line of Jean Genet's long poem, 'Le Condamné à Mort':

> Le vent qui roule un cœur sur le pavé des cours.

The first thing to realize (and Sartre, who provides the introduction to the book *Our Lady of the Flowers*, a translation of *Notre-Dame des Fleurs*, seems not to realize the first thing) is that Genet virtually *is* Baudelaire. Not that he's – except in the deliberate re-reverberations – an imitator. *Being* Baudelaire means being as original as Baudelaire.

Genet is, however, a Baudelaire of the twentieth century, with the result that he writes finer poetry in prose than in verse. 'Le Condamné' is tinged with Reading Gaolery. It is the prose of *Notre-Dame des Fleurs* which defines and realizes the most cogent mythology of poetic images since Baudelaire's.

Our present disesteem of writing (or, more probably, our insensitivity to it) is bitterly shewn up by the fact that the English reviewers, approaching Genet as a philosopher or sociologist, have scarcely noticed that he is a *writer*. This must be quite personally bitter to Bernard Frechtman, who has made a brilliant translation into North American: clever when need be – when Genet, seemingly defying translation, writes of himself as 'exilé aux confins de l'immonde (qui est du non-monde)', Mr Frechtman

47

ingeniously comes up with '. . . the confines of the obscene (which is the off-scene of the world)' – but rising above cleverness to positive inspiration as constructions and paragraphs pursue and come excellently close to Genet's very cadences.

The fashion for scarcely noticing Genet's imagery is set by Sartre, who stands sentinel over this edition. His long introduction consists, in fact, of a chapter from *Saint Genet*. True, Sartre has a section headed 'The Images'; but he turns out to mean things like Genet's 'will-to-unify', his desire to '*verify* his *conceptualism*' and his Platonism – which 'one would think . . . at times' is 'a kind of Aristotelianism'. He is noble and grotesque, this impresario who, apparently blind and deaf to the talents of his prodigy, none the less intuitively – and generously – feels there is *something* in him, and goes stumbling round and round while he tries to think what on earth it can be – and above him swoops, sombre and solid, dazzling in smoothed black-and-white marble, a vast, wing-spread, baroque angel of death.

Genet's images are all of death: to be more precise, all of funerals. His is the imagery of the *chapelle ardente*. It is in seductively beautiful bad taste. The book starts with a shrine of faces torn from the illustrated papers, photographs Genet has stuck to the wall of his prison cell and whom he takes as his imaginary lovers when he masturbates on his 'straw mattress, which has already been stained by more than a hundred prisoners'. The faces make a 'merveilleuse éclosion de belles et sombres fleurs' – funeral flowers. All these handsome young men are murderers who have been executed. The heads, cut off in the photographs, have in fact been cut off by the guillotine. For 'the most purely criminal' of them Genet has made frames – 'using the same beads with which the prisoners next door make funeral wreaths'. The form of the book is the stringing together of images into a funeral wreath. It is part meditation, part memory, part masturbation. The whole book is, according to Sartre, 'the epic of masturbation', but epic it is not: it is *not* a story, though it includes episodes of masterly narrative; and it is about sainthood, not heroism.

It was not Sartre who invented Saint Genet but Genet himself – in this book where he is identified with the character named Divine: 'it is my own destiny ... that I am draping (at times a rag, at times a court robe) on Divine's shoulders'. 'Tantôt haillon, tantôt manteau de cour' ... but always female. Divine is an 'il' always referred to by Genet, and almost always by her own thoughts, as 'elle'. Only when the narrative goes back to her country childhood does Divine become for sustained passages 'il', the boy Lou Culafroy; once she has come to Paris, where she lives as a prostitute, sharing her attic with a succession, an Attic frieze, of handsome 'macs', Divine is in permanent travesty: literally so in a phosphorescent night-scene at a drag party, and always so in imagination. On the very evening of her arrival in Paris, she rises from a café table 'wriggling in a spray of flowers and strewing swishes and spangles with an invisible furbelow'. Having established that Divine is himself, Genet goes on: 'I want to strip her of every vestige of happiness so as to make a saint of her' – to make, in other words, Saint Genet, a saint in drag, like a doll-madonna in a lacy skirt.

Calling the book an epic, Sartre has ignored the information Genet gives: 'I raised egoistic masturbation to the dignity of a cult.' The whole nature of the book is stated in the *cult*. Genet does everything, strings his entire wreath, with – in the Catholic sense – an intention. His opening sequence is strung from a clutch of homosexual men with flowering, frocked or girlish names – 'Mimosa I, Mimosa II, Mimosa mi-IV, Première Communion, Angela, Monseigneur, Castagnette, Régine': a 'long litany', he calls them, 'of creatures who are glittering names'. These he threads (they themselves are carrying 'wreaths of glass beads, the very kind I make in my cell') into a black funeral cortège in the rain. (The priest leading it becomes lost in an erotic fantasy.) The funeral is of Divine herself. The book begins and ends with the death of Divine: in between, she has betrayed herself to the police for a minor crime, and a murderer has betrayed himself and been executed. Genet is having a masturbation fantasy, but he is also dedicating an altar. As he tells his readers at the start, as he meditates before his shrine of assassins, 'c'est en l'honneur de leurs crimes que j'écris mon livre'.

Erroneously Sartre hammers at the idea of a medievally-minded Genet. Genet's imagination is, however, essentially post-Counter-Reformation. Divine's death-blood is 'revealed with dramatic insistence, as does a Jesus the gilded chancre where gleams His flaming Sacred Heart'. The cult of the Sacred Heart was not observed before 1648. Like the 'litanies' and the 'ex-voto dans le goût espagnol' of Baudelaire's vocabulary, Genet's is the overblown, peony-sized language of devotional flowers that did not come into existence until faith had been challenged from outside. It is necessary, precisely, to *counter* the Reformation: you must screw your eyes tight shut and *exclude* the outside world – that is, you must *induce* the images.

As it happens, faith has been emptied out from this tight-shut imaginary world. The idiom of rites and cults is employed to induce a state not of grace but of mind. Genet says nothing about religion, either way. It is his literature, not his faith, that is Catholic. Linguistically and psychologically, the idiom of the erotic and the idiom of the religious are the same; therefore the two are wholly the same for Genet, who is utterly a psychological linguist. When Notre-Dame des Fleurs is – 'la bouche ouverte en o' – penetrated by Mignon ('sa queue lourde et lisse, aussi polie et chaude qu'une colonne au soleil' – the cult practised by Genet's imagination is a phallic cult), he is Bernini's St Teresa pierced to the heart of ecstasy by an angelic spear. Indeed, one of Divine's lovers is a soldier named Gabriel, whom Divine addresses as 'Archange'. And Genet is an ecstatic – 'mon âme de cambrioleur extatique'.

The *cambrioleur* is interchangeable with the saint. The confessional is interchangeable with the outdoor lavatory in the country (in both places 'the most secret part of

human beings came to reveal itself'), where the boy Culafroy 'roosts' ('juché sur le siège de bois'), listening to the
rain on the zinc roof and aggravating his 'bien-être triste'
by half-opening the door and letting himself be desolated
by the sight of 'the wet garden and the pelted vegetables'.
An invocation may in psychological fact be offered in-
terchangeably to a divinity or a lover. (We all pray when
we are in love – to the person we are in love with.) When
Divine is arrested on the boulevard, she is singing the
Veni, Creator, of which the essential item is the *Veni*, the
inducing of a presence.

For Genet, the essential item throughout is that rites
are performed with an intention, gestures are, like masses,
offered – to whom or for what is not the point. First,
induce the images. When they exist to be dedicated, you
can offer them to whom you will, just as the 'thou' of a
sonnet can be equated with whatever initials you care to
write at the top.

Sartre is for once construing Genet aright when he
traces to masturbation fantasies the peculiar technique of
Genet's storytelling, whereby he admits to making up his
characters as he goes along, dithers visibly about what
form to make them up in, signals in advance that such a
one will presently enter the book and sometimes leaves
the reader free to imagine the dialogue two of them have
on meeting. He is a resurrectionist, treating his characters
like zombies. Even Divine, who is Genet, has to be led by
the hand by Genet – to sainthood: 'Et moi, plus doux
qu'un mauvais ange, par la main je la conduis.'

The technique of ushering his characters into the book
permits Genet to create effects of baroque theatricality, as
if he were seeing them on to the stage down a *trompe l'œil*
avenue. Thus 'Our Lady of the Flowers here makes his
solemn entrance through the door of crime, a secret door,
that opens on to a dark but elegant stairway'. This is
trompe l'œil indeed, for, having effected Notre-Dame's
entrance into the book, Genet continues 'Our Lady mounts
the stairway . . . He is sixteen when he reaches the landing'
– and at this point the narrative merges into actuality; the

character is on a real landing, about to knock and go into a room and murder an old man.

The rhythm, whether of masturbation or of Genet's prose, is designed to induce the images to take on enough solidity and durability to be dwelt on. And it is interesting that Divine's sex life is lived almost wholly in the imagination. It is not only that most of the narrative is the product of Genet's masturbatory fantasy: even when the narrative steps wholly inside the play-within-a-play, the sexual acts with the partners do not replace masturbation, on which Divine still depends to 'finish off'. The acts with others do not advance Divine towards direct sexual satisfaction; they serve to consolidate and sharpen the contrast on the images – so that in the end the images almost take off into a detached sex life, coupling and enjoying the process on their own.

Indeed, it is the images rather than the characters that Genet animates, which is why he is more poet than novelist. The independent life he charges them with is so erotic that it is no surprise to find them combining; they themselves are the population of a gallant and promiscuous society. Since the images combine, Genet's mythology is metamorphotic. (This is a point Sartre half-takes; he keeps using the word 'metamorphosis', but without much direction.) In two sentences heavy with nineteenth-century – with Second-Empire – baroque, Genet explains: 'For low masses are said at the end of the halls of big hotels, where the mahogany and marble light and blow out candles. A mingled burial service and marriage takes place there in secret from one end of the year to the other.'

That is the conjurer's *trompe l'œil* of the author who speaks of 'my taste for imposture, my taste for the sham, which could very well make me write on my visiting cards: "Jean Genet, bogus Count of Tillancourt".'

The furniture actually lights and blows out candles by one of Genet's most poignant devices, a fusion of images in the melting-moment of a syntactical plus semantic paradox. When Divine and her men leave the all-night drag party, 'the dawn was tight, a little tight, not very sure of itself, on the point of falling and vomiting'. And when the boy Culafroy waits in the moonlit country garden, among the washing, hoping the man he loves will come, 'La lune sonna dix heures'.

Indeed, the entire language of *Notre-Dame des Fleurs* is built up from the grammatical metamorphosis of 'il' into 'elle'. From this flowers the *argot* which is used only by 'males'; for Divine to use it would be as unseemly as 'whistling with her tongue and teeth ... or putting her hands in her trouser pockets and keeping them there'. Even so, the metamorphosis is never fixed. It is a film Genet can run backwards at will – and which he does, when, with the meticulous and dispassionate love of an early watercolourist recording exotic fauna, he describes that bizarre change of life that comes at thirty, the moment when a beloved crosses over and becomes a lover. Suddenly Divine does whistle, does put her hands in her pockets – until she discovers that after all she 'had not become virile; she had aged. An adolescent now excited her ...'

I feel tolerably sure that this particular metamorphosis has a reflection in Genet's own name. Is it his real one? He hints that it is not – by calling his boy-self Culafroy, where I suspect, but cannot wholly decipher, a pun. Genet is not the man to have failed to contemplate – to make a cult of – his own name, whether real or assumed. Take him straight and he is *un genet*, a jennet, a Spanish horse – an image, to his mind, as another of his transformation scenes demonstrates, of virility: but put, as surely his own imagination often does put, a circumflex on the second *e*, and he becomes some kind of flowering gorse or furze – a companion to all those secondary characters named Mimosa who weave a decorative and feminine garland through the book.

Genet plays paradoxes and transformations not only with words and single images but with myths: Christian (Mignon goes to church to pray 'Our Mother Which art in heaven ...') or pagan (Genet is *so* homosexual that for him it is the sailors who charm the Sirens) or both. Were

Genet making Divine not in his own but in the image of
the men who commanded his love, he would make her
'with flat and polished cheeks, heavy eyelids, pagan knees
so lovely that they reflected the desperate intelligence of
the faces of the mystics'.

Charmingly unexpected, and unexpectedly charming,
Words is Sartre's autobiography up to the age of ten.

At moments you might think he *wrote* it at ten, instead
of fifty-nine. He seriously confesses that 'even now' he
reads thrillers 'more readily than I do Wittgenstein'. If
you retorted 'Don't we all?' you would shatter a genuine
innocence. Sartre truly believed that other people were
'the grown-ups'.

However, Sartre is no mere *naïf*. He has a *talent* for
naïveté. If he is ignorant of one or two things which everyone else knows, he says several which everyone knows but
no one else has pointed out. 'I was a fake child', he writes
– 'J'étais un faux enfant.' Only now that he's said it about
his own childhood does one recognize that of course all
children are fakes; indeed to be a child is to be in a false
position. *Words* performs a tremendous feat. It exposes
the pretentiousness of childhood.

An only child whose father died before he was weaned,
Sartre was brought up in his mother's family, the Schweit-
zers. (Sartre is second cousin to Albert Schweitzer.) His
mother's love for him was strong but her personality faint.
She was, like all the adults in the family (and like Sartre's
book), dominated by Sartre's grandfather, a hearty, bilingual Alsatian whose first name Sartre gives indifferently
as Charles and Karl. The grandfather, however, chose to
be dominated by his infant grandson.

The difficulty was that a child has no positive personality to impose. The only response the child could make
to his grandfather's infatuation was to play the part of a
child. He also played the beauty, at least till his curls were
cut off. (Even the grandfather, Sartre sardonically reports,
was disconcerted by having taken a 'little wonder' to the

barber's and bringing home 'a toad'.) He played the infant prodigy – and there is a passage of lovely buffoonery in which he is briefly sent to school and withdrawn because the teachers fail to see his prodigiousness. Occasionally, he plays not a rôle so much as the droll: he reads *Madame Bovary* and, to his mother's objection 'But if my little darling reads books of that kind at his age, what will he do when he grows up?', brings out the *enfant terrible* reply 'I'll live them!' Eventually he accepts the rôle of genius elect, the boy predestined to be a famous man of letters.

And in fact the whole story is told through Sartre's relation to literature. The excellent translation (by Bernard Frechtman, the brilliant translator of Genet's *Our Lady of the Flowers*) was published in the USA as *The Words* and in Britain correctly as *Words*. By '*Les Mots*' Sartre obviously means just 'words'. His account of his infantile relation to them is divided into two parts, 'Reading' and 'Writing'. In the first, he pretends to read before he can – and thereby accidentally teaches himself to; he stage-manages little dramas in which the adults come on him devouring Corneille; his true but surreptitious literary diet, furtively supplied by his mother, consists of garish weekly instalments of blood-and-thunder. In the second part he becomes a prolific novelist. His novels merely rearrange his favourite reading: 'I . . . had not the slightest difficulty in reinventing . . . the exciting adventures that I read in *Cri-Cri* . . . I loved plagiarism, out of pretentiousness.'

It is the nullity of childhood which Sartre evokes with, I think, more exactitude and concentration than any writer before. He speaks of 'the insipid happiness of my early years' and of his self, his very Ego, as '*nothing*: an ineffaceable transparency'. Had there been siblings or a father – someone to be irritated with him for his monstrousness or even his mere existence – he might have been so occupied in replying to their impingement, in *producing* those reactions whereby a child's personality is eventually formed, as never to catch himself in the act of having no personality. As things were, Sartre was 'idolized by all, rejected by each'. His circumstances were a warm and loving nest which none the less did not pack him tightly. There was a layer of vacuum between him and them, a space into which everyone invited him to expand and express himself – the space in which he had room to realize that he had nothing to express and that he was a vacuum himself.

Having caught himself being a child, Sartre deep-froze the perception. He discloses that what he did with his childhood between finishing it and starting his autobiography was to forget it.

It is a literary advantage that Sartre is not in a position to write about 'childhood'. (I can't help feeling that if he could he would.) He *has* to concentrate on the particulars of the unique Sartre childhood. The result is that *Words* is in a different artistic category from all the words previously written by Sartre – all those words that have made him the writer of some of the most interesting books of our century but never one of our century's most interesting writers. Up to now, even in that almost tightly open-and-shut classic case *Huis Clos*, there has always been some faltering of Sartre's faith in the power of an artistic structure to stand up on its own. Fiction, since it escaped from the duty of pointing a moral, has been autonomous (existentialist, if you like); there is no *point* to *Madame Bovary*. Fictions are elaborate metaphors from which the other half of the equation has been stealthily removed; they are still metaphors, but not metaphors *of* anything. Sartre has always seemed to me a novelist and playwright who (no doubt working against Sartre the philosopher) is stealthily trying to put the other half of the equation back – to make the situations of his particular heroes *mean* something in terms of a universal human situation.

The felicity of *Words* is that, as it is not fiction, Sartre is not called on to feel faith, and that he cannot refer to a universal child situation. There *is* a sounding-board to which his particular hero is continually referred, but it is another particular – the adult and, especially, the literary Sartre. Sartre traces the influence of his early reading on his later writing: sometimes explicitly – he says the blood-

and-thunder conventions explain why Oreste, in *Les Mouches*, is so quick to take decisions; sometimes implicitly – when he says 'I was afraid of . . . crabs', he presumably has the hero of *Les Séquestrés d'Altona* in mind; once without knowing what he is doing – only in the light of his 'I had an epic mind' can I explain Sartre's indeed epic blunder in applying the word 'epic' (*anything* would have fitted better – 'limerick' would have fitted better) to Genet's baroque masterpiece *Notre-Dame des Fleurs*.

By interleaving the adult and the child writer in himself, Sartre seems to be working through – and reshaping – his acceptance of his literary vocation. 'Like all dreamers,' he says, 'I confused disenchantment with truth.' Did he make the same mistake about his own talent? Knowing that his grandfather foisted the rôle on him, and that he accepted it pretentiously, did he conclude that his literary vocation was itself false? He almost persuades you that it was. His 'One speaks in one's own language, one writes in a foreign language' is the remark of a born teacher, not a born writer. And yet: Sartre knows what only a writer can, the secret of *why* writers write (a secret impenetrable even to Freud): he wrote, he says, 'in order to be forgiven my existence'.

Nowhere is Sartre's distrust of art (or of himself as artist) more plainly figured than in the texture of his prose. As he correctly says in *Words*, 'I'm not a gifted writer . . . I've been called laboured'. But even in the labouring of his prose I've always suspected an imposture. Sartre has been like a man with a flair for dressing well who (confusing disenchantment with truth) insists on wearing stained tweeds on the assumption that dandyism must be false or frivolous.

In *Les Mots* Sartre, for, I think, the first time, made something like a dandy's use of the French language. He beat out a few hasty, terse near-epigrams. Hiding inside the text of the book there is a charming fairy-tale whose hero is a little boy with a talent for *naïveté*. In Sartre's version of the fairy-tale, what the little boy points out and what no one else has dared to say is that the *little boy* has no clothes on.

John Horne Burns

I should guess that only a few of those old enough to remember will, in fact, remember the literary splash that went up in 1947 (in the United States) and 1948 (in Britain) about a book of fictional or fictionalized sketches called *The Gallery*. The author whom it made briefly famous, John Horne Burns, was from the United States. He was in his early thirties and newly out of the army. The subsequent career of his reputation illustrates not so much the viciousness as the whirligig irresponsibility of literary circles.

Horne Burns's next publication (in 1949) was a longish novel, *Lucifer with a Book*, set in a private school – a sort of American Gordonstoun. Horne Burns satirizes it in broad, lethal swathes and with hideous hilariousness. I've heard it suggested that this exposure of an American institution from the inside (Horne Burns himself had done some teaching both before and after the war) was more than the United-States critics could forgive. However, most of the British critics, who presumably were less tender on that point, seem to have shared the American response to the book: a response of furious attack or even more furious silence. The next novel, *A Cry of Children*, appeared in 1952; it was again set in the United States but written in Italy, where Horne Burns had gone to live. About this one, his British publisher, David Farrer (of Secker & Warburg), presently commented to Horne Burns by post that it 'must hold the record for being the most savagely and *unfairly* criticized novel of the century'.

In 1953 Horne Burns, still in his thirties, died at Florence. His name, already out of fashion, began dropping out of remembrance. His books trickled out of print. However, their posthumous reissue and reissue as paperbacks is an act of justice not only to Horne Burns but to the public. In my very serious opinion, John Horne Burns was by far the most talented, and the most *attractively* talented, North American novelist to emerge since the war.

Probably it was the war which occasioned the misunderstanding in the first place between Horne Burns's talent and his critics. Literary criticism had spent the war years asking (unanswered): 'Where are the war poets, the Rupert Brookes of this generation?' When the war was over, it made decent allowance for the fact that most novels take longer to write than most poems and then started asking: 'Where are the war novelists?'

The Gallery must have looked a plausible answer. Its title is a pun: the book is both a gallery of portraits and a series of meditations on the Galleria Umberto Primo which was the Piccadilly Circus of American soldiers in Naples. However, Naples is only a thematic centre. The sketches cover North Africa as well as Italy – they follow, indeed, the route taken by the American army and Horne Burns with it.

This obvious factualness made it easy to misread *The Gallery* as a book about war reported in tranquillity. Moreover, Horne Burns carried many of the marks to be expected in the much expected soldier-prose-writer. He obviously felt he would burst if he could not explain what the war had really been like, as opposed to what films and magazines had made it look like. He was bitter with awareness of the irreconcilability of army-reality with civilian-reality. He even loosed at the civilians a few of the blows they half wanted in order to cancel their sense of being in debt.

The very form of *The Gallery*, a discontinuous narrative with different characters for each section, helped it to pass for naturalistic reportage: a soldier's experience of war *is* episodic. At the same time, this broken surface concealed that in conception the book was unified; thematically considered, it was a novel; and the conception was a large one. Horne Burns was working on a wide social front: he was concerned not with American–Italian encounters but with the interpenetration of two civilizations. More important-ly, he was working in depth as well. His psychological theme was the agony of a personality obliged to choose between two systems of reality. That these came out, in his first book, as the irreconcilable realities of the army and of civilian life was an historical accident – an accident which made it possible for the critics to appreciate his brilliance but appreciate it superficially. Almost inevitably they overlooked that what they had, to the credit of their discernment, got hold of was not a war writer but a writer. What distinguishes *The Gallery* is not its 'brilliant observa-tion' (though that *is* brilliant) but its imagination.

This is not to deny that Horne Burns was one of the writers who use (but imaginatively and psychologically use) their own experience. His fiction after *The Gallery* continues to invoke the war as a climactic experience, a fence which now lies behind his characters but which they can never forget having surmounted. The hero in each of his novels is a 'veteran', that word which the American language, with perhaps a stab of unconscious cruelty, pins on young men returned from wars as though to label them as prematurely superannuated – 'pins on' much as if the general, in affixing the medal, were to stab the pin into the soldier's chest. To David, the hero in *A Cry of Children*, the parish priest remarks: 'Permit me to tell you, my son, that the Navy has changed you. You used to be such a spiritual little fellow.' Guy, who in *Lucifer with a Book* has come from the army to teaching and finds himself out of patience with the school's hypocrisies and, presently, its reviving militarism, carries from the war a scarred face – not, I think, a corny symbol of a scarred soul but something more subtle and also more psychological, the equivalent, in fact, of an hysterical symptom: the scar is an engrained wince.

On the naturalistic level, this use of the war and the figure of the veteran is simply the novelist's justifiable opportunism: it made for socio-historical plausibility.

More and more, however, it becomes clear that it was by socio-historical accident that the war coincided with the climactic experience in Horne Burns's and his heroes' past. More and more he used his veteran-figure to express not just the serviceman's resentment of the civilian but a passionate and poetic individual's indignation against society. No doubt the moment when his development became conspicuous was the moment when the critics parted from him. The motif had, however, already been enunciated in *The Gallery*, where a second lieutenant of the engineers foretells a society where 'The queer, the beautiful, the gentle and the wondering will all go down before a race of healthy baboons with football letters on their sweaters.' ('Queer' is to be taken in both senses.)

The second lieutenant who says this has been accosted in a bar in Algiers by a corporal. (It is possible that both figures represent Horne Burns, who entered the army as a private and became an intelligence officer.) The lieutenant turns on the corporal in a way that brilliantly sums up what must, I think, have been Horne Burns's own state of mind during his army service. 'How', the lieutenant asks without preliminaries, 'do *you* know you're in Algiers? Or for that matter what proof can you give me that you're alive?'

The same state is described in one of the meditative 'promenades' which interleave the 'portraits'. The 'I' of these is not necessarily, and sometimes obviously isn't, Horne Burns's literal self, but I am sure it is Horne Burns's autobiography the 'I' is writing when he says: 'I got lost in the war in Naples in August, 1944. Often from what I saw I lost the power of speech. It seemed to me that everything happening there could be happening to me. A kind of madness, I suppose. But in the twenty-eighth year of my life I learned that I too must die.'

He was right in supposing it a kind of madness. (More than one sketch in *The Gallery* touches on madness.) It was, I surmise, an extreme neurotic prostration precipitated by traveller's trauma – which is no doubt more acute in armies but may overtake even tourists; indeed, it is too little appreciated how many people are slightly mad while they are abroad. Horne Burns is describing the moment when the alienness of a foreign country becomes depressing, and the knowledge that 'I too must die' verges on the suicidal determination that I *will* die. 'I got lost' – or I lost my 'I'. The self suffers the loss of the very cell walls which keep it distinct from the outside world; everything which happens out there 'could', as he says, 'be happening to me'. It is the sensation of unreality which comes from being unable to choose between two realities.

The realities are irreconcilable because they are shocked by each other. Horne Burns was shocked by Italy (as he would eventually have been in any case, by the sensual life *somewhere*): but his imagination made him, by sympathetic adoption, an Italian, and he was then shocked by America. The American habit of 'Having Sex', says the 'I' of *The Gallery*, 'began to strike us in Naples as being so cold-blooded ... we came to look upon this ... ejaculation without tenderness as the orgasm of a frigidaire'. The wince scarred into the veteran Guy's face is the wince of a puritan – but a Janus-puritan, shocked both ways.

Horne Burns's dustjackets were reticent about his history ('born in 1916 in the State of Massachusetts') and his friends not much better informed. I can't even guess (I never met him) whether his native puritanism was Catholic or Protestant. (I *feel*, but without evidence, that it was Irish). One of the 'I's in *The Gallery* remembers back to a childhood which includes the First Baptist Church: yet in *A Cry of Children*, where all the main characters are Catholic or lapsed, Horne Burns not only saturates his characters' behaviour and thoughts with a sly Catholicism ('Dear Father Rushton had a grace that only schismatic Anglican clergymen are said to have') but strings the images of his own writing like the beads of a rosary – 'The trees on Brimmer Street looked like arthritic nuns, too numb with orisons to get off their knees, with a veil of sleet and ice weighing down their old heads.' Perhaps Horne Burns was (an Irish fatality) the child of a mixed marriage: the most rollicking section of *The Gallery* concerns the friendship of a Catholic and a Baptist army chaplain, who pussyfoot round each other in their dog collars and combat boots as they try both to score off and to be tolerant of each other, and who end in comradely disaster in Naples over drink and a prostitute.

With most writers, one *could* guess. Non-Catholic writers seldom *dare* to conceive Catholic-reared characters from the inside. But the distinguishing mark of Horne Burns is the boldness of his imagination. It is comparatively easy to have the courage of one's convictions, to *think* nothing human as alien from oneself. It takes artistic genius to have the courage of one's imagination.

Horne Burns can plunge not just into female minds but into a female institution, the staff common room of the girls' school which is twinned with the boys' school in *Lucifer* – and he brings it off with tremendous funniness but also tremendous finesse. Homosexual himself (a friend described him to me as 'the most *committed* homosexual I have ever met'), he is quite honest about the homosexual themes in his books and yet does not hesitate to create heterosexual love. No more does he hesitate to create Italian minds. As a theme, Italy figures to him much as it did to the early E. M. Forster, as the instinctual life in opposition to nordic puritanism: yet compared to Horne Burns's, Forster's Italians have the pretty impossibility of shop-window dummies, small men's size. Horne Burns's imaginative daring shews even in his naturalistic observation. Even an overhear depends on the auditor's *daring* to catch the words: just as one often finds after saying 'I beg your pardon?' that one has in fact heard after all. Horne Burns dared catch the whispers of the unideal in the nation he had made his ideal. He captures for instance – and for ever – the leaden over-elaboration, the fatigued classicism, the nineteenth-century comic-paper quality of Italian jokes, when he records a snatch between two prisoners of war cleaning the latrines in an American army VD clinic: 'Sa che cos'è la sifilide? Un'ora con Venere e dopo sei mesi con Mercurio.'

From passively suffering, as a neurotic affliction, that

dreadful feeling that what happens to others might be happening to oneself, Horne Burns developed a positive – an artistic – comeback on life, plunging his imagination into *being* his characters. He draws in bold strokes, sometimes caricaturing, sometimes creating a sort of farce of indignation. He is bold in scale. He is not afraid to bid to be universal; and he can justify his bid because the depth of his penetration into alien minds lets him use colossal perspectives. Perhaps the finest of all the sketches in *The Gallery* is the one about a queer bar in Naples, a meeting place for the homosexual soldiers of six nations. Without losing the immediacy of this, to him, most immediate of subjects, Horne Burns has chosen the one artistically right – and at the same time the boldest – method of 'placing' it in a perspective both ironic and compassionate: he displays it through the eyes of the middle-aged Italian woman who – in demi-innocence – runs the place. Again, in *Lucifer*, where Guy's struggle with the school is so palpably Horne Burns's own struggle with schools and post-war America at large, he builds so steep a perspective (an historical one, this time) that the book as a whole resembles a dizzily high historical monument. It is done by the simple bravery of opening the narrative in the nineteenth century and in the mind of an old, dying, high-born American Protestant spinster – in accordance with whose will the school where Guy eventually comes to teach is founded. Conversely, the final paragraph of *The Gallery* creates a geographical perspective, down which the book recedes from the reader – the reader sails away from the book: 'Outside the Galleria Umberto is the city of Naples. And Naples is on the bay, in the Tyrrhenian Sea, on the Mediterranean . . .'

Such perspectives served Horne Burns, who always composed on two planes, as great conduits of poetic illumination down which his two planes comment on and contrast with each other. The positive come-back of the affronted puritan in him was to achieve a compassionate irony about sex; and as a baroque designer he missed no chance to redouble his irony by exploiting the theme of bisexuality. The sergeant in *The Gallery* who has got into the hellish

VD camp ('We ain't interested in making these shots pain-
less', says the GI who gives him his first injection) through
a love affair with an Italian girl finds himself solicited by
an American sergeant on the staff of the camp.

A similiar design is worked out with more elaboration
in *A Cry of Children*, where Horne Burns takes off into so
towering a flight of imagination as almost to leave the
naturalistic plane out of sight below. The events retain just
enough probability to make the characters' sensations of
nightmare terrifyingly convincing. The dialogue falls into
cadences not quite naturalistic, yet flexible enough to *represent* natural speech – an idiom, a Racinean convention, of
Horne Burns's own evolving (though I think it may be
developed out of a self-mocking manner of talk current in
New York: a not dissimilar idiom is used in a novel which
was published in Britain in 1963, *Textures of Life*, by that
excellent United-States writer Hortense Calisher).

The centre of *A Cry of Children* is the love between
David, a rich ex-Catholic pianist (there is evidence in all
the books of Horne Burns's musicalness), and Isobel, a
poor, ex-Catholic slut. This centre is, however, im-
mediately fissioned by the fact the Isobel has a twin, Fred.
David is in divided relationship – in relationship not to
each of the two, but to the twins. His love for Isobel is
shadowed by an unrealized homosexual love for Fred: but
that in its turn is shadowed by an erotic cruelty between
the two men, which is realized when David deserts Isobel,
and Fred, to punish him, straps him to the bed and beats
him up.

It is easy to guess that Isobel and Fred were created by
Horne Burns's consciously splitting a single original; in
the early part of the book Isobel reads like a woman
faked-up out of a character originally conceived as a boy.
But if Horne Burns has faked it he has done so for no
dishonourable reason: indeed, through artistic necessity.
Isobel had to be a woman if the design was to be brought
to the point of perfection where the east wing could echo,
ironize and set off the west wing. And Isobel's agony, by
the end, though most particularly female in circumstance,

has refined away everything that is not simply and universally human. David has not only deserted her but made her pregnant. The abortionist she goes to is a lesbian Negress (who advises her, as the seducing sergeant in the VD camp advises *his* patient, that the way to keep out of trouble for the future is stick to homosexuality). Losing her nerve, but too late, Isobel has to be strapped to the operating table, in echo of David's being strapped to the bed. Her child is taken from her almost by an act of rape. The death-dealing operation is equated with the act of love. ('I don't think I care to say goodbye to Madam', Isobel says when she is well enough to leave. 'She don't care to see you either, honey,' replies the assistant. 'It's like a one-night stand.') The ultimate irony at the end of all the perspectives of Horne Burns's imaginative world is a kind of bisexuality not between homo- and hetero-sexuality but between sexuality at large and death. The monumental design proves – which may be true of all baroque designs – to be a tombscape. From its superb height one is looking, chilled, into the lesson Horne Burns learned 'in the twenty-eighth year of my life', that 'I too must die'.

If it comes to my mind to see Horne Burns as a designer in marble, it is probably because his was an inherently streaky talent. No one could deny that he offered tooth-holds to the critics who savaged him. The idiom he evolved for *A Cry of Children* occasionally melts into an anticipation of Salinger-like babytalk. Towards the end of *Lucifer with a Book* Guy sometimes takes on a goody-goodiness which makes the narrative resemble those last five minutes of flag-stirring patriotism which used to be tacked on to otherwise sophisticated Hollywood films. Indeed, in certain lights the handsome and athletic Guy, like at least one of Scott Fitzgerald's autobiographical heroes, forces home to me that it may be the utmost handi-cap to a novelist to be good-looking. Like Fitzgerald (there are fleeting similarities to be caught in their artistic personalities, too), Horne Burns was handsome – and, unlike Fitzgerald, large. What must have been even more

69

disconcerting to him is that he looked, in every meaning of the word, normal. To meet, I have been told, he was just 'an American college boy' – perhaps one of the 'healthy baboons with football letters on their sweaters'.

However, although the critics were right, they were also utterly wrong. It would be impossible to have the good in Horne Burns without the thin streak of bad. Both come from the tremendous generosity of his imagination – which was like the sort of mouth called generous: capable of great tenderness, but also of slobbering over. He is not one of those simple cases where a classical novelist is waiting to be let out of his own tomb of flesh, one of those cases whose prototype is George Eliot, who could be transformed tomorrow not merely into one of the greatest (which she is already) but one of the most perfect novelists – by any competent editor with the arrogance to set up his own judgment against hers and strike out all those paragraphs of non-fiction she littered through her novels in the puritanical belief that imagination was not enough. Horne Burns had the courage, and sufficiently overcame his puritanism, to commit himself to his imagination, even where it was artistically unsafe. His prototype (and he is of a stature not to make the comparison belittling to him) is Dickens.

No doubt Horne Burns's streaks grew larger as his achievement grew larger, just as the pattern on a balloon gets larger as you blow the balloon up. I have every reason (that is, both a knowledge of the nature of Horne Burns's talent and a knowledge of the critic's perceptiveness) to accept David Farrer's judgment on Horne Burns's last – and never published – novel, namely that it contained both his best and his worst writing. I have not seen this last novel and indeed do not know if the typescript still exists. I know of it only through David Farrer's courtesy. It was set in Italy and concerned a love affair between an Italian, Mario, and a North American, Helen (who in the course of the story visited a fictionalized Bernard Berenson); it was called *The Stranger's Guise*.

Horne Burns's United-States publisher rejected this

novel. Secker & Warburg sent him back the typescript with David Farrer's detailed recommendations for revising it. From Italy Horne Burns replied: 'Perhaps I'm getting older, for I find the report 98 per cent just in its findings . . . I know now precisely what must be done . . . I cannot afford another scalping this time . . . No, your remarks were not harsh. I should prefer to be brought up short by my editors than by the critics and the public.' He said that he hoped to finish the final draft 'within a month'. But within a month he was dead.

From the distance of England his friends could not make out the circumstances of his death. They were certain it was tantamount to suicide, but uncertain whether he literally killed himself or drank himself to death. He had lately had a disastrous love affair with a Florentine boy.

I do not for a moment imply that Horne Burns was killed by a reviewer's paragraph. It seems likely he had suffered a return of the neurosis which had attacked him during his army service in Italy. Since his distress lay precisely in a dissolving of that narcissism which attaches a person's instinctual love to his own Ego, and so attaches him to life, it is possible that some public appreciation of his writing (appreciation equals love) could have tided him over. But it could have been only tiding over. That his distress came from his own personality is clear from how much of his love affair with death is pre-implied in his books, even as far back as the first book and even down to details. *The Gallery* already contains the theme of neurotic drinking (the one part of the American myth expatriates seem unable to shake off with the soil of America). The meditative 'I' in *The Gallery* seems, when he writes 'There'll be Neapolitans alive in 1960. I say, More power to them', not to expect to live to 1960 himself. Even the Florentine boy was foreordained. He enters the queer bar in the Galleria in Naples on the last page of the section, in the company of his lover, a Captain Joe. Their entrance sets off a rough house in which the clientele smash up the bar for ever.

We have, but John Horne Burns hasn't, lived on. May he not be one whose name was writ in water.

Antonia

My novel *The Finishing Touch* has had several manifestations in hardback and paperback. When GMP published it in paperback in 1987, I realized that I was at last free to describe its genesis in my imagination and that its genesis might now have a wider resonance than among the handful of art-historically knowledgeable people I had mentioned it to earlier. I therefore wrote an introduction to the 1987 paperback edition.

I have only once put a deliberate portrait of a real person into a work of fiction, and *The Finishing Touch* is not that work of fiction.

For reasons which I could trace for a psychoanalyst but which anyone else would find tedious, my temperament is anti-autobiographical. In addition, since I write both fiction and non-fiction I find it simpler to keep my fiction imagination, where you are required to invent, quite separate from my non-fiction imagination, where you are always checking dates and quotations in order to avoid accidental invention.

I do not dislike or despise autobiographical novelists: who could dislike or despise Marcel Proust? I cannot, however, be one of them, any more than I can be one of the symphonists. And to a very small extent I do despise the common academic assumption that *all* novelists are autobiographical.

What a novelist invents is seldom an entire country or an entire substitute reality, though I have made shots at doing both. Something, however, in your real reality sets your imagination going. After the fiction is written, you can, on lucky days, remember or deduce what the spark consisted of, especially if it is fixed in your mind by some external event.

In that sense I owe *The Finishing Touch* to a conjunction of chicken pox and the fact that I married an art historian.

I think that it was in 1963, when she was six, that Michael Levey's and my daughter Kate caught chicken pox. She did not feel ill for more than half a day. Michael and I escaped worry but not the tiresomeness of keeping a perfectly well child at home for what seemed weeks until she passed the infectious stage. I discovered that Michael had not had the disease during his own infancy. I counted on his good health to shield him. I had not had chicken pox, either; but I already had a rational inkling, which a doctor has since confirmed, that I possess a natural immunity to it.

Kate had passed the infectious boundary and gone thankfully back to school when Michael developed chicken pox. He was beyond the advisable age and for three or four days the disease made him feel deeply ill. He simply lay in bed suffering, itching and sweating.

He recovered to the point of getting up. He could not, however, go back to his work at the National Gallery or even into the local shops because he was still a source of infection. He refused social life, even with friends who had safely had chicken pox, because most of the spots were on his face and he supposed them to make him look a good deal worse than they really did.

What did impair his looks was that he thought it wiser not to shave lest he decapitate a spot by accident and cause a pock-mark. He grew a scrubby and scratchy beard, which disobligingly refused to hide the spots but circumnavigated them, leaving them sticking up like peaks; and that made him even further disinclined for company.

My immunity held through proximity to the two invalids. I felt an itch, but it was spiritual. My imagination had been seized with a novel. I yearned for time, extracted from shopping and from escorting Kate to and from school, to write it. And, since Michael was deeply bored by staying at home in the company only of a preoccupied wife, I yearned to put the finished manuscript into his hands in the hope of amusing him.

I met that private deadline by a couple of days. As a matter of fact, I that year sent a parcel containing two novels to my publisher, who decided to publish the briefer quickly, in the same year, and the longer in the next year.

As a result of Michael's assistant keepership, as it then was, at the National Gallery, I met most of the personnel of art-historical London. My part at such meetings was chiefly that of spouse/appendage, a part that leaves plenty of time for observation. What sparked my imagination to a new novel were the meetings Michael and I had with the head of an institute that taught art history. Michael occasionally lectured there and more often attended lectures by colleagues. On such occasions the head often invited us for a drink afterwards in his flat on the top floor of the remarkably elegant building that housed the institute.

Like the building, its head was remarkably elegant: in word and gesture alike. His tastes were – and that, too, was in keeping with the architecture – austere, both in relation to works of art and in food and drink. When he dined with Michael and me he became the only person I have met to refuse champagne. When we had a drink with him, which happened more often, his hospitality was multifarious but his own consumption nil.

He talked to us freely and happily about his bilingual (English and French) upbringing as the son of a British clergyman resident in France. There was much, it later became clear, that he did not say to us. Yet we became good, though never intimate friends with him. He belonged to an older generation than ours and generously forgave us our ignorances. He spoke in a charming upper-class drawl that was neither an affectation nor quite an Edwardian relic, and he seemed for ever on the verge of utter exhaustion. He was tall, slim and very nearly beautiful.

Whatever was concealed, there was no concealment,

from us or anyone at the institute, of his homosexual affiliations. His flat on the top floor was separated from, but not impregnable to, the rest of the building. Whenever we went there, the evening was tattered by brief incursions of young men introduced by first name only, who might have been sailors or might have been students of Poussin and were very likely both. They would put to him practical and domestic problems ('The mustard you said would be in the cupboard on the left isn't') and he would wave a hand, dismissing not the person but the problem. Practical matters he seemed to find gross. To bend his attention on them he seemed to find impossible; the mere suggestion that he try seemed to drive him nearer than ever to the point of exhaustion.

When Michael and I came home after one of these visits we would decide in the course of discussing it that the presence of the young men in that not very self-contained flat was deliberately induced as a protective barrier, on the lines of the flitting sylphs in *The Rape of the Lock*, against more dire incursion by one of the women in the institute, who included both undergraduates and teachers, who obviously and sometimes explicitly considered him sexually desirable.

The institute, which has its handsome home in Portman Square, is the Courtauld Institute of Art. Its head was Sir Anthony (and then suddenly just Anthony again) Blunt. Everyone in the Institute had always addressed and spoken of him just as Anthony anyway.

What my imagination did, when it picked him up by the scruff of his neck, was change his sex and make him the headmistress of a finishing school for girls. Perhaps it was the hell he had imagined for himself. I notice that through all metamorphoses he retains his excellent, virtually native French and something of his adumbrated liking for sailors. He also retains his name. *The Finishing Touch* is the title supplied by my publisher, which I agree to be a better title than the one I originally wanted, namely simply *Antonia*. My publisher sent someone to search reference books for finishing schools in the south of France.

Infected by the all-fiction-is-autobiography fallacy, he was convinced I was slandering some institution where I had myself been educated and was not to be persuaded of the truth, which is that I have never set foot in a finishing school and would not know where to seek one.

Lisbon: City as Art

If you must have an earthquake, 1755 is the year to have it: when you rebuild, you will get a full-blown eighteenth-century city. That is what happened to Lisbon. Yet, by a freakish and unjust oversight in the development of taste, Lisbon is not very famous.

People do, of course, tell you to go there, but usually for things – climate, nightlife, cheapness – which can be found equally well elsewhere and which do not particularly attract the visitors who would appreciate what is unique to Lisbon. So, because the people who would notice it seldom go there, it remains almost unnoticed that Lisbon, the city itself, is one of the most ravishing works of art in Europe.

Like the clever child whose first act of intelligence was to be born of the right parents, Lisbon shews its prime artistic inspiration in its choice of natural setting. A handful of hills drops steeply to the estuary. Down them tumbles the city, like a harvest of exotic fruits from a cornucopia.

The Lisbon style is exotic – and yet homely. It is fantastic, far-fetched and yet, in a chunky way, slightly comic: like a pineapple. As a matter of fact, the pineapple is a sort of patron fruit to the city. Cartloads of pineapples are hauled up the streets, baskets of them stand about on the quays like bollards. Like other southern places, Lisbon is full of dark, stone shops opening abruptly on to the narrow pavements and shewing the wasteful over-specialization that goes with under-employment. Often you pass one that sells nothing but pineapples. Peering into it from the bright Lisbonese sunshine is like peering into a pool where the goldfish have dived deep. It takes a moment before the cut-glass facets of the fruits define themselves and you realize you are looking at a row of pineapples, each hanging on its individual string from the ceiling, as glowing as Chinese lanterns in a grotto.

The exotic strain in Lisbon is a direct response to a Moorish history, an overseas empire and the brightness of the light. Almost every surface in the city is patterned. Most house fronts are tiled, so that they look trellised by some intricate green-and-blue or green-and-yellow flowering plant. Those not tiled are washed in colour – often deep, porous-looking terracotta or midnight blue. Many houses wear curving iron balconies like a flutter of black lace at the bosom. Lisbon pavements are mosaics (the first requirement of a woman visitor is a pair of flat-heeled shoes), and often the pavement is patterned with arabesques of black or dark-green on white. The most splendid of all the patterned pavements is a promenade down the centre of the grand avenue (one of the most truly grand in Europe) da Liberdade. In the lay-bys of this broad path, the mosaic underfoot spells out the names of national heroes, but down the middle it sticks to the abstract curlicues of high fantasy, as though some very dotty but very grand grand-duchess had dipped her train in ink and gone swishing down the hill.

Extravagance of decoration is matched by extravagance of flora and, indeed, fauna. The grapes in the shop windows are as big as plums, the cat who throws himself into your lap when you sit down in the shoe shop (to buy a pair of flat-heeled shoes) as heavy as a baby. Lisbon is so used to being fruitful that it treats even bread as breadfruit: the rolls come to table each wrapped in its own tissue paper, which is made into a bag by a moustachio-twist at each end – the way oranges are sometimes wrapped in England. Wherever there is space for it, Lisbon has a park; failing that, a tree: failing that, a flower shop. Palm trees as well as fantasy duchesses march down the Avenida da Liberdade, alongside a continuous stretch of water-garden carried from level to descending level by waterfalls twelve inches deep – which serve to separate the family of white swans on one of the upper reaches from the black swan who, usually from inside his house, exotically rules a lower one. In the Estrela garden the blossom trees are of deep purple, and the waterscaping here is subtle, sunken, almost secretive. On the edge of the pool, two storks preen each other – and the whole garden rustles with large, unusually tame and unusually bright-coloured peacocks.

All Lisbon seems to play with water. Cars are always being hosed in the streets; the streets themselves are hosed on Sunday mornings and are so steep that the water shoots down them as if down a roof; the stone walls of the very flower shops drip from the repeated hosing of their merchandise.

The water games seem echoed by the sounds of the Portuguese language, which is bolted and shuttered against foreigners. You feel that if you tried to learn it you would gain no Portuguese but lose whatever you might have hard-won of Italian, French or Spanish. To the eye comprehensibly latin (though the eye takes a second or two to work out that a shop calling itself *chique* is claiming to be *chic*), it is in pronunciation inimitably Moorish. The -*ash* and -*ish* endings of its words resemble the curly tails of arabesques or the lapsing plumes of a fountain; and their splashing in conversation round you as you walk through the street creates for the imagination a fairy-tale Arabian water-garden.

Lisbon's more-than-Vuillard riot of conflicting patterns would be intolerable but for two more-than-saving graces. One is natural: the light. Lisbon's is both a southern and a seaside brilliance. It is a city where you are always either going down to the sea or up to an eminence from which you can see the sea. The whole place is drenched in a brightness thrown off by the sea's crumpled silver-paper surface. Perhaps patterns conflict only when you cannot really see them. In Lisbon the glaze on each tile gleams individually, like the separate scales on a lizard in some meticulous eighteenth-century zoological illustration. At the same time, because you are always going up and down, and from darkness into brightness, the city continually composes theatrical effects. Look up a narrow street, and across the top, in full sun, is the façade of a house or – which in Lisbon is usually plainer – a church, lying flat against a vivid matt-blue sky: it is pure backdrop, and the faint sea breeze which is always animating Lisbon seems to send a ripple through the canvas. Look down the same street, and the three-dimensional effect is so exaggerated that it seems it must be created out of cardboard. Halfway down, as if placed by the designer to impress the perspective on you, you will usually see one of Lisbon's black-shawled, black-stockinged women balancing a tray on her head while she talks to an invisible interlocutor in a dark doorway. (It is presumably by some Middle-Eastern convention that only the women use their heads for portering: the men put their burdens on their shoulder.) The whole scene is like a blatant demonstration, a figure from a trigonometry textbook.

And mathematics, in a sense, is Lisbon's other redeeming grace. The eighteenth-century genius was for the architecture not just of buildings but of cities as wholes. The Marquês de Pombal, who was Joseph I's Minister at the time of the earthquake, took the opportunity to let in air and light – a deep draught of (in the most literal sense) the Enlightenment, of gracefully reasoned mathematics – to what must have been a medieval-cum-Renaissance fortress town. From the top of a belated monument, an Edwardian, rather ugly but impressive Pombal presides over his grand avenue. The avenue is flanked now at the top by modern buildings, further down by nineteenth-century ones – some of which writhe in the last spasms of the rococo manner; theirs is the statuary and the engraved glass of an *art nouveau* rococo, dedicated in spirit to Sarah Bernhardt. But though its components may degenerate, the structure of an eighteenth-century town plan is as immune to decay as the bone structure of a face. (It can of course be massacred: but that needs a fully capitalized philistinism, such as has destroyed London.) The grand design of the grand avenue marches on to the huge Praça Rossio, now agreeably strident, commercial and neoned.

This breaks into a perfectly logical grid of small, fashionable shopping streets planned by Pombal even down to what sort of goods were to be sold in each street. One of them now contains a bank whose name seems to epitomize, charmingly, humanity's attempt to have the best of both worlds – the Banco Espírito Santo e Commercial de Lisboa.

The downward streets – the entire plan proceeds downhill – of this network lead into the Praça do Comércio. This is that rarity in Lisbon, a large flat space – a square of which three sides constitute a commanding eighteenth-century palace, colour-washed in a beautifully melancholy green. The fourth side is the sea. In the centre of the square, as though emphasizing that this is one of the few spots in Lisbon where you could exercise a horse, there prances a massively and curvaceously rococo equestrian statue.

In the beautiful arcades of the green palace, the paint peels. Above that, the small, economical political posters – which in Portugal means government exhortations – peel too. (The last sentence is explained by the fact that I made my first visit to Lisbon, but by good fortune not my last one, and wrote this description of the city before the beautiful flowering of political democracy in Portugal.)

· When you leave the lee of the palace and approach the sea, the wind hits you, and with it melancholy. The quays are as desolating as a disused railway station. You become aware of the close connexion – and the geographical distance – of Brazil. The wind wafts in a dream of empire and at the same time howls for an empire lost. It is on the quays that Lisbon is most conspicuously an international port and an imperial city – and also a provincial market town. In every Lisbonese café a man hopes to be allowed to polish your shoes: down on the quays five or six such men eagerly run at you, carrying their little footrests-cum-seats. There are trays of depressing doughnuts, and of wiry toys; and a rack of cheap, horribly innocent paper books and magazines.

It is provincial – yet imperial. If you go in spring, before winter clothes are discarded, you see men in coats or half-coats with sheepskin collars. They look as if they had just dismounted after a day's work on a South American ranch. In spring, too, the roast-chestnut barrows are still in the streets, putting you in mind of even older empires. The charcoal fire in the belly of the barrow has for a chimney what looks like half an unglazed earthenware pot. Sometimes the pot has been cracked and then riveted and wired together again. It might be any age, last year's pot or three thousand years old. It is dateless in material and in shape – a vast breast. It might be Cretan, Phoenician, Carthaginian.

Lisbon has not, as a matter of fact, forgotten Carthage. Inscriptions over shops – or, sheerly, the telephone directory – shew that Aníbal is a not uncommon first name.

On both sides of Pombal's design for Lisbon rise cliffs of townscape on which even the eighteenth century could not impose symmetry. What it did do was to crown the most salient height with the Estrela church, which is Lisbon's unacknowledged masterpiece, and make over to the baroque style the interior of churches on other eminent points, like São Roque and São Vicente, whose fabric dates from the sixteenth century. In São Vicente the bottom altar on the right takes flight into a brilliant baroque fantasy of Saint Michael. In São Roque the deep-recessed side-chapel of Saint John the Baptist glows with Portuguese extravagance which was in fact designed by Vanvitelli, in Italy; the whole thing was, by another kind of Portuguese extravagance, shipped bodily in 1710.

It is advisable – and in any case probably inevitable – to get lost on your way to São Vicente, because that is the one sure method of penetrating the huddled poor quarter you would never find if you looked for it. Lisbonese slums teem much more *privately* than Italian slums. Their hermetic life seems not so much European as North African. Even the distinguishing marks of a Catholic culture are not visible. No shrines hang on the corners of houses, and there is none of that black scurrying of priests across sunlit squares that one knows from Italy, because the Portuguese constitution separates church and state and priests do not walk abroad in their *soutanes*.

You can go up Lisbon's inhabited cliffs by cruel long hauls of shallow steps or by sharp stone staircases as sheer as those in a ship; by a sort of funicular tram; by ordinary tram – I say 'ordinary', but the tramlines look like the tracks left by virtuoso skiers. Or you can take a taxi. The steepness of Lisbon defeats even the Lisbonese. It is one of the few cities where the inhabitants actually use their taxis themselves, and taxis are not only cheap but available, since they cruise all over the city.

Lisbon also has buses, and for English visitors these have a peculiar disconcertingness: they are green-and-cream double-deckers, of the kind you see in the Home Counties. There is a comic *bizarrerie* about waiting beside a palm tree for what is to all appearances the municipal transport of Slough. Indeed, whether through the proximity of Gibraltar, through being, as the British are taught to say whenever Portugal is mentioned, 'our oldest ally' or simply through the sympathy of one bereaved imperialist power for another, the Portuguese have adopted several appurtenances of English life. One of them is the umbrella, much more freely carried by Portuguese than by most South European men. Even more surprising, if you are used to the continental habit of hiding the public telephones in cafés and letter-boxes in walls, is the sight of red-and-cream telephone-boxes like English ones, and free-e-standing vermilion pillar-boxes on the English model but just a touch, I think, slimmer.

The easiest way-in to the idiom of Lisbon's architecture is via the museum. Actually, the Museu Nacional de Arte Antiga has much else to offer: an introduction to the painting personality of Domingos António de Sequeira, a Portuguese and lesser, but all the same fascinating, Goya, and an international collection containing several fine pictures (an Allori 'Rest on the Flight', two Tiepolo *bozzetti* and a Cranach 'Salome') and two masterpieces. It fits in with the long historical wrangle between, on the one hand, the two nations of the Iberian peninsula, and on the other the states that were to resolve themselves into the two Low Countries that the famous Bosch triptych of the

'Temptation of Saint Anthony' should be in Lisbon. But it seems by the merest act of flotsam that a Piero della Francesca should have fetched up there – until you see the picture, which is of a full-length Saint Augustine: round his cope runs a frieze of biblical scenes, almost of tiles, that one would swear had been designed in the Portuguese taste.

That taste itself the museum sketches in a collection of objects removed from churches: painted wooden statues two foot in height and charmingly dumpy in design; weighty black-and-gold altars like dressing-tables for a queen in mourning; and an entire chapel rescued bodily from a convent, gleaming with tiles, grilles, marble, and wrought and beaten gold-coloured metals. You have to stand and let yourself, too, be wrought and beaten upon for a minute before you become versed in the idiom. All baroque and rococo are acquired tastes, but in Lisbon particularly so because, compared with the style of Salzburg or Bavaria (or even the delightfully eccentric and localized version of it in which Prague is built), the Lisbon style is provincial. Where they offer a porcelain airiness, Lisbon offers the splendour of a piece of chunky jewellery.

Eighteenth-century Lisbon was provincial even while it was going up. The earthquake was one of the great news items of eighteenth-century Europe, nutshelling for a sceptical age the whole problem of the benevolence of God. It was a San Luis Rey of the old world. But Portugal's own response to its disaster, as Voltaire shews us by the bitter fun he pokes in *Candide*, was considered by the rational rest of Europe to be old-fashioned, superstitious and stupidly cruel.

The cruelty, at least, is no longer part of the atmosphere. I expect a Portuguese bullfight is as vile as any other teasing of animals, but – since Pombal's time – they do not kill the bull. An English visitor can be shamed by the poster in the airline office which allures tourists to Britain by a photograph of a foxhunt. We British still do kill the fox. The style of Portuguese art and of Portuguese religion

(for whole tracts of history the two are pretty well synonymous) is worlds away from the torments of Spanish art
and religion. The two countries are as different in *feel* as
in language and landscape. Lisbonese churches are almost
without paintings of tortures, deaths and atrocities, without crowns of thorns. Indeed, you could tour them without
discovering that the Christian deity is male. Lisbon is ruled
over by a baroque madonna.

Remaining provincial, Lisbon itself has not caught up
with the revolution in taste which would nowadays make
its architecture high fashion if it were known to the rest of
Europe. The Victorians never acquired the acquired taste
for baroque or rococo. Even in 1913, when avant-garde
spirits were beginning to turn back to the eighteenth century, Baedeker was being bad-temperedly dismissive about
Lisbon's churches. Lisbon seems to have got stuck in Baedeker's period. (It has, for example, too few open-air cafés
for the number of Lisbonese who would like to sit at
them. As though it still thinks the open air perilous to
health, its café life is Sickertian, conducted in great rooms
with bare floorboards, round, marble-topped tables and
billiards upstairs.) Tacitly agreeing with Baedeker, Lisbon
thinks its churches not worth mentioning or even recording. You can search the shops in vain for a postcard of the
outside – let alone the harder-to-photograph inside – of
the Estrela, though you may have a hundred tinted pictures of the madonna at Fátima, who looks as though she
had been produced by Max Reinhardt, and almost any
article you can name executed in cork. And when you ask
the friendly taxi-driver for the Estrela he will – once he
has understood that by 'Estrela' you mean what is in
Portuguese pronounced something on the lines of
'Ishtreller' – assume you want to visit the garden, not the
church.

Although it suppresses the harsh and bloody episodes
of the Christian story, Lisbonese church architecture has
not gone soft. The bright white façade of the Estrela, a
dizzying fantasy of pierced towers which half-masks the
marvellously mannered and elongated dome in the centre

of the building, is the apotheosis of sugar-icing architecture: but it is markedly *hard* icing – wedding cake, yet with an undertaste of the funeral feast. Most of Lisbon's churches are sad. Their expected exoticism (in any country where 'kiosk' is spelt *quiosque* and pronounced 'key-oshk', you would expect the churches to be half mosques) goes so far as to hint at the barbaric. Besides the Moorish, there is a touch of another important influence in Portuguese history – a suspicion, in the deep-hanging metal lamps or in a banister which rails off part of the nave into a sort of flat gallery, of the synagogue.

Once your eye is in, it sees that decoration is not used to conceal or merely cover surfaces, but is put into the service of structure, defining and emphasizing forms. One of the brilliant devices of the Lisbon church is to push the heaviest decoration outwards, into the side-chapels, so that each separate jewelled construction is isolated in its own recess and glows individually like Lisbonese pineapples on their individual hooks. The shapes of Lisbonese architecture are themselves the shapes of a baroque madonna; it is an architecture of heavy bosoms. Lisbon never quite took off into the elegance of the rococo. Provincially, it stayed behind, weighted down not just by its provincialism but by sorrow. If Lisbon has almost expunged Jesus Christ from Christian iconography, it has thereby isolated the sadness of the bereaved and ageing madonna. What is truly barbaric about its style is that all its beating of metal is inspired by the same emotion as the beating of a breast; its extravagant habit of piling marble with lapis lazuli and then encrusting it with enamel is equivalent to the behaviour of a provincial widow who piles one outmoded, slightly absurd but splendid garment on top of another as a gesture of mourning.

Knowing the prejudices of 1913, you might guess from Baedeker's remark – 'the fitting up of the interior is ornate rather than artistic' – that the interior of the Estrela would in fact be the most beautiful of all Lisbon's interiors. But neither acquaintance with Lisbon nor reading Baedeker by contraries could tell you in advance that the interior, tall and almost gaunt, is – for all its lacertine splendour of marble – poignantly austere.

The Estrela (officially the Basílica do Santissimo Coronação de Jesus – the high altarpiece is of the flaming Sacred Heart) was designed, apparently in imitation of an earlier eighteenth-century Portuguese church, by Matheus Vicente and Reynaldo Manuel, and was built between 1779 and 1796 to the orders of Maria I of Portugal, who was fulfilling a vow, her prayers for an heir to the throne having been answered. Her lovely and chilling black-and-white tomb stands to the left of the high altar. 'The Latin inscription', says Baedeker, 'is curious'. He seems to have been being malicious. Perhaps he meant the Latin is curious. The inscription itself, though of almost unreadable length, seems a conventional eulogy of Maria's piety and her zeal in building the church, plus a mention of her residence on the other side of the ocean.

As a matter of fact, she died there; her body, following the Portuguese fashion for shipping things, must have been brought home. The personality of Maria I epitomizes the tragi-comedy of Lisbon. I see her as a sub-Goya, a Portuguese Goya – in fact, a Sequeira – queen: short, rather clumsy, her rouge unequally apportioned between her two cheeks. I see her leading in Brazil a life of Ronald Firbank exoticism and exaggerated Catholicism, being fanned by pious maids with pampas grasses. She was the daughter of Joseph I, the earthquake king, and she married her father's brother. Perhaps it was the superstition that such marriages are infertile that made her feel it necessary to pray for an heir. Baedeker does not bother to mention that an altarpiece on a side-altar at the left of her church shews the queen, dumpy and sweetly pie-faced in the bottom right-hand corner, beholding in the top left-hand corner a vision of a madonna almost as dumpy as herself. During the Peninsular War the Portuguese royal family took refuge in Brazil. Maria I died in Rio de Janeiro in 1816. She was eighty-two, and had been mad for the last twenty-four years.

When you leave her church, cross the road and go to

the Estrela garden opposite, you seem to catch an echo of her gauche poignancy in the squawking of the splendid peacocks under the palm trees.

Don't Never Forget

Mozart's letters allow one to be, in imagination, Mozart. Professor Deutsch's indispensable volume allows one to inhabit an eighteenth-century Europe briefly visited and nonplussed, as in a baroque miracle, by Mozart's angelic genius.

Professor Deutsch's technique of biography-*vérité*, or documentary biography, previously exercised on Handel and Schubert, is deadpan. After a section of 'antecedents', he starts straight in on January 1756 and the registration of Mozart's baptism and proceeds to print chronologically (and here in versatile translation) every extant document (except, of course, the Mozart family's letters, though he includes even those when they are official petitions) with a bearing on Mozart's life. Selection has been done only by time and chance. The mortar between documents is minimal and scholarly: the provenance of each and (which is sometimes the Deutsch volume) its place of first publication, plus bare references and cross-references.

Professor Deutsch notes, after the baptismal entry, that Mozart was born on St John Chrysostom's day, but leaves the reader to notice for himself that, in the continental fashion, it is the later Christian names that count, the two by which Mozart called himself being preceded by the saintly sleeping partners Joannes Chrysostomos, and that the Amadeus (presumably given in compliment to the godfather) is registered in its Greco-Latin form, Theophilus. The multilingual wordplay characteristic of Mozart's mentality (and no small part of his operatic aptitude) seems predicted at his very christening.

This technique is, of course, no substitute for insights into Mozart, though it may provoke new ones (or indeed corroborate old; I, for instance, who have traced the influence of *Hamlet*, which Mozart discusses in a letter, on *Don Giovanni* as well as on *Idomeneo*, the context in which he instances *Hamlet*, am charmed to find a contemporary reviewer of the opera saying: 'Mozart seems to have learnt the language of ghosts from Shakespear', and Constanze affirming, after his death, that her husband had been 'well acquainted with Shakespeare in the translation').

But this story, simply as a story, is all the more vivid for not being told but left to be observed. So is the external, meetable personality of Mozart: a little man with a pale face, blue (by one account) eyes, a tenor singing voice, a passion for billiards, a childhood dread of the trumpet, an adult dislike of the flute and the harp (why a flute was nevertheless indispensable as the magic instrument in *The Magic Flute* I trace in the 1988 Libris edition of my book *Mozart the Dramatist*), a talent for drawing, the habit of 'always playing with something, e.g. his hat, pockets, watch-fob . . . as if they were a clavier' and a propensity (which reminds us that he belongs to the world of Jane Austen) for exchanging with his friends inscriptions in albums. Indeed, in one album Mozart (perhaps, as Professor Deutsch suggests, because he was then considering another trip to England or perhaps through the sheer Anglophilia declared in his letters) chose to write in (foreigner's) English: 'Don't never forget your true and faithfull friend.'

In newspapers, advertisements for sheet music, posters, programmes, title pages of libretti, Professor Deutsch's readers get news of Mozart through much the same media as they would if it were all happening now. They experience the shock of his death at thirty-five ('I was beside myself for some considerable time', wrote Haydn) and, from closer to, the agony of Mozart's knowing that he was dying ('I have the taste of death on my tongue') and dying poor. Professor Deutsch's scholarly note bites all the more ironically deep for correcting the legend: 'It was not a pauper's funeral, but the cheapest available.'

Then follow the wads of officialese through which Con-

stanze eventually secured a widow's pension, and details
of the concerts in which she toured to raise money: sometimes she and her sister Aloysia, whom Mozart had been
in love with before his marriage, sang his music; once the
six-year-old Wolfgang stood on a table in Prague to sing
the *Vogelfänger* song his father had written for Papageno.
That was how the world paid the artist whose creative
imagination and intelligence are perhaps the best vindi-
cation the human species could push forward were the
evolutionary process to ask why humanity should not be
scrapped and replaced. Don't never forget.

Miss J. Austen

A horrid and slanderous cult-idol still stalks our landscape. It purports to represent an early-nineteenth-century novelist to whom her devotees attribute such qualities as 'gentle irony' and 'playful wit' and (presumably in a spirit of gentle irony or at least playful wit) the name 'Miss Austen'.

This cult evidently wants to emphasize its subject's spinsterishness. The mock respect implies that, though she is a stickler for the prissier proprieties, her sternness, like the scratches of her wit, goes no more than skin-deep. The cumulative suggestion is of a rather dear village schoolmistress – a figure who has no connection whatever with the late-eighteenth-century novelist Jane Austen.

True believers in the autonomous imaginative worlds of great fiction resent literary cults, which they intuitively – with the very hairs on the nape of their necks – interpret as acts of crypto-philistinism, whose unconscious purpose is to distort the artist they consciously laud. The distortion is exactly symbolized in the coy, quaint fashion for speaking of Jane Austen as Miss Austen. By a beautiful malign irony, 'Miss Austen' is a howler. In English usage, only the eldest daughter of Mr and Mrs Smith is Miss Smith, later-born daughters being Miss Mary Smith, Miss Emily Smith and so on. Jane Austen naturally followed this rule both as an author and as a real-life member of the upper middle class. Indeed, she relied on it, or a shorthand version of it, to introduce and identify as sisters two of the characters in a fictitious letter (in the juvenilia), where the heroine records: 'Miss Greville laughed but I am sure Ellen felt for me.' In superscribing her own non-fiction letters, Jane Austen correctly reserves 'Miss Austen' for her elder sister Cassandra; conversely, when she tells John Murray where he may write to her, she specifies that he direct his letter 'to me (Miss J. Austen), Chawton, near Alton'.

Miss J. Austen is the opposite of the cult-figure. She would have made a lamentable schoolmistress. For one thing, and not such a tiny one as it seems because it may well be a symptom of anarchic forces in her temperament, she couldn't spell. R. W. Chapman gallantly footnotes his edition of her Minor Works with the explanation that her spelling of 'Freindship' is 'not eccentric'. Yet though orthography was still fluid at the time there is a suspicious fatality whereby Jane Austen seems always to pick on the spelling – 'peice', 'veiw', 'greif', even 'teizing' – which was *not* to become the correct one; and the point seems settled against her by her own inconsistency in 'Catharine', where she spells the heroine indifferently with an *ar* and an *er*.

She would not make a schoolmistress because she is in fact a grand, programmatic educationalist; and far from being rather a dear, she is the most sardonic person who ever set pen to paper.

The earliest scraps to which she set pen (and which she preserved in fair copies) shew that she was sardonic from further back in her history than any other writer whose history is known. She never had, like Gibbon, to deplore her adolescent enthusiasms; not even in childhood was her imagination costume-dramatic; its first literary act was to start straight in satirizing other people's romances. Those who believe great literature to be the outcome of a meeting between sweetness and light are refuted by Jane Austen. It was by the apparently 'destructive' method of tearing to bits the nonsensical content and the inflexible epistolary technique of the novels she read that she brought off, in the ones she wrote, the tremendous creative feat of fashioning the classic conventions of modern novels of morals.

The form is still – immensely – alive and its moral subject-matter datelessly the concern of all human beings who have to construct a morality for themselves instead of relying on a supernatural religion. The preoccupations out of which Jane Austen created the form were, however, those of the eighteenth century. She is an eighteenth-century writer in the sense that she is the novelist that century had been trying to produce all along. She is an educationalist in the same way as Rousseau or a hundred lesser propounders of ideal educations – as part of that supreme educational programme, the Enlightenment. Like every other eighteenth-century thinker from Pope to Sade, she confronts the problem that God, though he may be allowed, and was certainly allowed by Jane Austen, to have created, is no longer held to intervene in Nature, and yet Nature, instead of prompting a morality, is morally neutral.

She argues, by satire, for Natural as opposed to Affected behaviour, yet has to oppose sense to the nonsense – or society to the selfishness – of perfectly natural passions. She puts her heroines in the love-and-duty dilemma of the typical eighteenth-century operatic heroine – *Persuasion* is one long, saddened and beautiful love-and-duty aria. Since she neither believes in magic nor expects miracles to take place, she can release her heroines only by bringing them out at the end of a rigorous moral education. A Jane Austen novel is what its subtitle calls *Così Fan Tutte* (that other masterpiece of anti-romantic satire) – a school for lovers.

The nexus of these moral educations is domestic, yet Jane Austen is slandered if she is called either a miniaturistic or a naturalistic novelist. Her books are domestic in the sense that the *Oedipus Rex* is domestic. Her moral dilemmas are often drawn in precisely oedipal terms: the end of *Northanger Abbey* explicitly questions whether the story's tendency 'be altogether to recommend parental tyranny or reward filial disobedience'. A childish nonsense piece discloses no less explicitly the matters on which her fantasy played, though the fantasy is turned to the pointed literary aim of sending up the vogue for first-person (Fanny Hill, Moll Flanders) confessions: 'I murdered my father at a very early period of my Life, I have since murdered my Mother, and I am now going to murder my Sister.'

The metaphors of her adult work are less violent than those of Sophocles, but they cut as deep and are no less metaphors. For all their surface verisimilitude, her plots are too symmetrical for naturalism: her lovers emerge from her imbroglios paired as in high comedy or opera; her books are crystals, which she taps pitilessly apart with the precision instrument, developed in satire, of a remorselessly analytical intellect.

Though no naturalist, she is a realist and knows that remorse no more solves the real dilemmas imposed by Nature than trying not to disbelieve in fairies conjures fairies into being; and she is not so short of life herself that she has to lay on her intellect sparingly for fear of drying herself up. She harries her heroines to logical extremes, with the relentlessness of a great tragedian, though her flail is not sadness but irony.

Her heroines are capable of two sorts of response, which may reflect a manic and a depressive aspect of her own artistic personality. The *joie de vivre* which is sketched in Elizabeth Bennet, but with such uncertainty of tone as to carry the book to, though never over, the verge of vulgarity, comes to perfection, in *Emma*, in a sheer fountain of the Life Force which not even the author's just and unyielding realism could resist. But another group of her heroines can learn from their moral education only by sacrificing to it a part of their Ego. The sketch here is *Mansfield Park*, from which Fanny (or, indeed, Edmund) cannot emerge without turning into a prig. This depressive branch of her work culminates in the autumnal masterpiece of *Persuasion*, whose heroine grows not priggish but old. Perhaps in *Sanditon* Jane Austen was going to encompass both poles of her genius.

Jane Austen differs from her eighteenth-century predecessors only as Mozart differs from most of his: she was a better artist. She was not only intensely intellectual, as many eighteenth-century writers were; she was, as few of them thought it worthwhile to be, intensely literary.

It is by a prejudice that we compliment painters and composers when we call them 'painterly' or 'musicianly' but insult a writer by calling him 'literary'. By a still worse prejudice do we suppose that the 'domestic' experience of a spinster is too limited to produce great art. As a matter of fact, we are all domestic – the word is synonymous with 'civilized'. Only in some Hemingway daydream is domesticity exclusive to women, while men wander as free as bandits in a landscape. And in any case, we have learnt nothing from psychoanalysis if we do not yet know that the emotional material of great art is experienced by everyone in the most incontrovertibly 'domestic' period of his life – before he is five; and we have learnt nothing from art if we have not noticed that all the adult experience in the world avails an artist nothing if he cannot relate it to and draw on the earlier deposits.

Devotees of the false cult-idol are at their philistine worst when they quote the letter of 1816 where Jane Austen writes of 'the little bit (two Inches wide) of Ivory on which I work with so fine a Brush, as produces little effect after much labour'. Devout quoters regularly commit the solecism of not reading the letter written by the novelist they intend to adore. Jane Austen writes to congratulate her nephew on leaving school. He has lost two and a half chapters of the novel he is writing. Jane Austen is glad that, not having been in the vicinity, she cannot be suspected of stealing them, but says that she doubts whether, had she stolen them, her own work could be joined to the 'strong, manly, spirited Sketches, full of Variety and Glow' by the school-leaver.

The often-quoted letter is the letter of a supreme ironist who knows her own novels to be admirably professional works of moving and spirited irony. I think it probable that she is the greatest of all novelists.

The Box and the Puppets

Chapter 39 of *Vanity Fair* is entitled 'A Cynical Chapter'. In a sense – a sense I mean utterly as praise – *Vanity Fair* is a cynical book. Thackeray is a cynic who knows the price of everything – its price in human pain and disillusion – and who leaves the value of nothing unquestioned.

The image of Vanity Fair is a borrowing from *The Pilgrim's Progress*, where the Fair, an allegory of worldliness, is a market – not only for worldly goods but for worldly pleasures and honours. Thackeray's Fair, too, is animated by buying and selling. It is a place of trafficking. Men are for sale in the City or on the fashion or politics market, women for sale on the marriage market: as Thackeray comments,

a title and a coach and four are toys more precious than happiness in Vanity Fair: and if Harry the Eighth or Bluebeard were alive now, and wanted a tenth wife, do you suppose he could not get the prettiest girl that shall be presented this season.

Becky Sharp, having missed the chance to sell herself in marriage to a baronet (one who would himself like to buy a peerage), marries Rawdon Crawley in the hope that he will inherit his aunt's £70,000 – a £70,000 which every member of the Crawley family is hoping to lay hands on by selling the old lady his personal charm or his solicitude for her health. When she does die, old Miss Crawley leaves a small annuity to her companion Miss Briggs, who goes into well-earned retirement – only to be driven quickly out again:

Briggs tried to live with her relations in the country, but found that attempt was vain after the better society to which she had been accustomed. Briggs' friends, small tradesmen in a country town, quarrelled over Miss Briggs' forty pounds a year, as eagerly and more openly than Miss Crawley's kinsfolk had for that lady's inheritance.

With that sardonic backhand about Briggs' being accustomed to 'better' society, Thackeray refutes the whole concept of 'good', let alone 'better' society. The little history of Briggs' annuity slices through the social layers and exposes that, in Thackeray's view, big fleas have little fleas all the way down. Likewise, of course, up. When Becky becomes (or as good as becomes) the mistress of the Marquis of Steyne, Steyne believes he has purchased Rawdon Crawley's complaisance as a husband. 'My lord had bought so many men during his life that he was surely to be pardoned for supposing that he had found the price of this one.' As it happens, Steyne is mistaken: Rawdon Crawley is stupider than Steyne thinks. The innocent, in *Vanity Fair*, are innocent only inasmuch as they are stupider or more gullible than the rest. They are the ones who get sold. When Amelia Sedley throws herself away on the lightweight, unloving George Osborne (a portrait of an *homme moyen sensuel* even more telling, and far more economical, than Tolstoy's Vronsky), it is with no passionate affirmation of 'All for love and the world well lost'. Amelia is merely, supinely, duped. She no more embraces her destiny than her merchant father embraces holy poverty when he goes bankrupt and is (that persistent buying and selling motif) 'sold up'.

Whereas Bunyan's pilgrims are only passing through Vanity Fair on the way to the Celestial City, Thackeray's Vanity Fair is not only 'the world' in its allegorical sense but a closed world. His is the tragedy of an ironist; the tragedy which is half an abrupt joke and which can be so much sadder than tragic tragedy. If the values of this world fail, and Thackeray demonstrates that they do, the abrupt tragic joke is that there's no other world.

Not a ray of celestial illumination enters Thackeray's book – which is one of the hundred contrasts between

Thackeray and Dickens, whose chiaroscuro nightmares gleam with infernal, if not celestial, light. Thackeray has none of that sense of evil which Dickens expressed graphically, by making his evil characters *look* evil. The worldly Thackeray has a subtler and more sceptical appreciation of people's surfaces; where Dickens (in the photographic sense) blows up the surface, Thackeray penetrates it. Dickens's genius is to draw us down to a child's eye view; reading Dickens is to stand at knee height, looking up at people who have the monstrous big heads of caricatures. Thackeray's genius is to oblige us to see through adult eyes. He won't let us romanticize or prettify. The subject-matter of *Vanity Fair* is comprehensible to a child of fourteen; its tone can be caught only by the disenchanted.

Thackeray's vision is through an immensely penetrating lens but from an immense distance. One of the distancing devices in *Vanity Fair*, one that's often forgotten, is that it is an historical novel. It is a sort of more intellectual *War and Peace*. The story opens at a time when Thackeray himself was a baby; at the Battle of Waterloo, which gives the novel its halfway climax, Thackeray was still a month short of his fifth birthday. *Vanity Fair* was published, in monthly instalments, in 1847–8. Spiritually, however, it belongs to the time not of its writing but of its setting. Thackeray, chronicler of the Four Georges, was a man spiritually born into the eighteenth century, which he factually missed by eleven years. A political history of England in the eighteenth century is written in miniature (along with an almost Vicar of Bray story of the sycophancy and place-seeking and place-buying which went on beneath the grand political surface) in the very names in the Crawley family tree, where a Sir Walpole Crawley is succeeded by a Sir Pitt.

Vanity Fair gets its period detail not merely right but lovingly right – even when it is factually wrong: either Thackeray or Becky Sharp has made a slip when Becky, recounting her arrival as governess at Queen's Crawley, writes to Amelia: 'Sir Pitt is not what we silly girls, when we used to read *Cecilia* at Chiswick, imagined a baronet must have been. Anything, indeed, less like Lord Orville cannot be imagined.' Lord Orville (who isn't, anyway, a baronet – but Becky at this green stage of her career is sufficiently ignorant of baronets to expect Sir Pitt to wear court dress perpetually) is in *Evelina*, not *Cecilia*. But what is overwhelmingly right is that the schoolgirls should have read *a* novel by Fanny Burney – indeed, they would probably have read them all and, to be fair, would have (who wouldn't?) mixed them up; what is brilliantly right is the Jane Austenish syntax of 'imagined a baronet *must have been*'; what is almost movingly right in its sensuous, linguistic feeling for the period is that Becky ends her next letter by apostrophizing Amelia – like Keats to Fanny Brawne – as 'dearest girl'. Thackeray's invention is wonderfully historically-minded. Miss Pinkerton wears a turban (the pretentious old thing would like to be an English Madame de Staël); the very incidental music, as it were, the music mentioned in the book, is by Stendhal's idols, Mozart and Rossini; the charades by her participation in which Becky shocks her respectable in-laws might come direct from *Mansfield Park*.

Likewise it is, I conjecture, from the quintessentially Regency town of Brighton that Thackeray borrows 'Steyne' for his marquis. I imagine he intended the pronunciation to be 'steen', as it is in Brighton. Finely attuned to the period, Thackeray gives the marriage-hungry sister of the wife of his Irish Major O'Dowd the first name Glorvina. It was a name popularized in 1806 by a novel called *The Wild Irish Girl* by Sydney Owenson, who in 1812 became Lady Morgan and, under that name, lastingly famous. In my introduction (reprinted in 1987 in my volume of essays *Baroque-'n'-Roll*) to Routledge's republication of *The Wild Irish Girl*, I have tried briefly to trace Jane Austen's unadmiring response to the book and its heroine and the lapse in Thackeray's concentration that allowed him in a skid of the narrative to transfer the historically apt name Glorvina from the major's sister-in-law to his sister.

Thackeray's, like the Regency style itself, is built firm on the eighteenth-century Enlightenment. Thackeray has only to toss off a history-in-a-paragraph of the school where Lord Steyne places the younger Rawdon Crawley (presumably Thackeray's own school, Charterhouse – before going on to which Thackeray had been, like Amelia and Becky, at school in Chiswick), and he unconsciously speaks in Gibbon's voice, remarking that Henry VIII hanged and tortured some of the monks of the old foundation 'who could not accommodate themselves to the pace of his reform'. Time and again, Thackeray's artistic taste inclines back to the eighteenth century. In 1847 it was by no means obligatory to characterize as 'beautiful', which Thackeray does, a quotation from *The Rape of the Lock*. In contrast to the architectural taste Dickens reveals in *Our Mutual Friend* ('Smith Square, in the centre of which ... is a very hideous church with four towers at the four corners' – that is, Thomas Archer's church there, which was completed in 1728), Thackeray obviously admires 'the great filagree iron gates' and 'the narrow windows of the stately old brick house' in Chiswick Mall from which his story takes its departure; and by 'old' he means, if one may judge from the non-fictitious houses which survive in Chiswick Mall, dating from 1700 or 1730.

And, indeed, *Vanity Fair* itself is a literary equivalent to those London houses which went on right into the 1840s and 1850s being built in the eighteenth-century manner. Thackeray is the continuer of Jane Austen. Taking up her moral concerns (Thackeray is a moralist, concerned with good and bad, whereas Dickens is a supernaturalist, concerned with good and evil), and also taking up her nexus of young marriageable people who can be put through the formal permutations of a mating gavotte, Thackeray expands the social nexus on to further social levels and extends her moral pessimism into his own sharp despair. He continues her, moreover, in a quite literal way: by taking his story beyond the point, marriage, where she regularly brings hers to a stop. Thackeray achieves, between the lines of the Victorian literary conventions, a singular sexual frankness. When Becky and Rawdon elope, he manages to give us the unambiguous information that their marriage, though already solemnized, is not yet consummated. He lets us know unequivocally that George Osborne finds Amelia dull in bed. Continuing the story beyond marriage, he has continued it into disillusion. His narrative edifice rests on two great pillars, Amelia's marriage to George and Becky's to Rawdon Crawley. Both marriages, unlike Thackeray's structure, give way.

Moreover, when Amelia, at the very end of the story, marries again, her feelings of affection and gratitude towards Dobbin are already known to be much paler than the romantic, duped love she felt for her first husband: but for Dobbin the marriage is the attainment of the ideal he had yearned romantically towards almost since the book began: and he is disappointed. His disappointment is even known, no doubt disappointingly in itself, to Amelia. In almost the last breath of the narrative Amelia thinks to herself (and sighs) that Dobbin is fonder of their small daughter than he is of Amelia. Thackeray does not contradict her thought: he confirms it with the 'but' by which he introduces the disclosure that Dobbin, having achieved the marriage which represents his romantic heart's desire, is in that marriage moved less by passion than by tenderness and duty – 'But he never said a word to Amelia that was not kind and gentle; or thought of a want of hers that he did not try to gratify.' It is Dobbin's married plight which directly provokes the second question in that final groan of commentary where Thackeray asks: 'Which of us has his desire? or, having it, is satisfied?'

The entire book is daringly built on disillusionment suffered and scattered by the twin sources of the action, Amelia and Becky. Thackeray has dispensed, as Jane Austen never quite did, with the heroic ideal. (*She* still creates heroes who are halfway between the unromantic position of entertaining no illusions to be disabused of and the authoritarian position of being able sufficiently to master the young women they marry to prevent them from broadcasting disillusion.) All Europe lost its last, and indeed desperate, attempt at a hero and master when the glamour of Napoleon went up in cannon-smoke at Waterloo. But Thackeray has never subscribed to Stendhal's romanticism. *Vanity Fair* is, its subtitle states, 'a novel without a hero' (and, one might add, without a heroine either). It forgoes a hero even before it loses George Osborne on the battlefield, and he is already discredited and de-heroized before he is left 'lying on his face dead, with a bullet through his heart'.

Vanity Fair is a sequel to Jane Austen's œuvre by virtue not just of its formal structure, but of its analytical formal structure. The famous opening, where Amelia and Becky drive away from school into the world (into Vanity Fair) and Becky tosses her leaving-present, a Johnson's Dictionary, out of the carriage (by what I take to be another period accuracy but one whose significance – archaism? genteelism? vulgarism? – I cannot trace, Miss Pinkerton and her sister pronounce the word 'dictionary' as 'dixonary'), must be the most concentratedly pregnant acorn from which a novel has ever grown. The single kernel gives Thackeray at once his plot and his historical, ironical point. He is going to place the two female friends *vis-à-vis* two young men who were also friends at school (and again he manages to make plain the erotic quality in Dobbin's idealizing love for his handsome junior George); from this social nexus he will precipitate Becky, bouncing like a mis-hit ball out of her fiasco with Amelia's brother, into the higher social world of the Crawleys; the bankruptcy of Amelia's family and the near-rupture of her engagement with George having given him his quarter-climax, he will bring his two social worlds together, and assemble most of his main persons, at his halfway climax at Waterloo. Then the groups split up again. Since Amelia and the faltering in her engagement have provided the quarter-climax, it falls to the other pillar, Becky and *her* marriage, to provide the three-quarter one, which Becky does by her intrigue with the Marquis of Steyne and its dramatic detonation (which shatters her marriage to Rawdon).

At that point Johnson's Dictionary comes back into the story: Rawdon uses it to help him spell his challenge to the Marquis. But it comes in as no mere formal echo. It is not even confined, like the intimation of Anna Karenina's death by train which enters the book at the moment of her first meeting with Vronsky, to echoing within the personal psychology of one character. Tolstoy's train motif is pinned down only by Anna and in other aspects flaps loose – aspects in which it is arbitrary, occurring at what is merely the point where Tolstoy chose to begin the relationship. *Vanity Fair* could not have begun otherwise than with Johnson's Dictionary. When Rawdon has recourse to it, he is falling back on the old Johnsonian rules and ideals, the *gravitas* and gentlemanliness of Johnsonian England. It is just these Johnsonian rules and ideals that Becky flings away at the start of her career and of the story; and it is not only George Osborne but Johnsonian England, eighteenth-century England, that was killed at Waterloo.

Vanity Fair has one of the most perfect, least forced, skeletons in the whole repertory of novels. The beauty of its structure is inextricable from the intellectual content of its structure. Whereas Tolstoy in *War and Peace* deploys his narrative strategically – a general responding *ad hoc* to the ground he has to cover – and impresses us by sheer size and sheer naturalism, Thackeray *uses* his lovely symmetrical structure for analytical purposes. Becky, as an adventuress who can swarm up and tumble down in social level, not only serves to stitch together the several milieux of the plot but actually and dramatically demonstrates the social fluidity of commercial England. The generations of Sedleys, Osbornes and Crawleys are spread out not simply to impress and move us, as they do, by the sheer human processes of ageing and breeding, but to allow Thackeray to explore causes. Unremitting analyst, he anticipates psychoanalysis itself, probing whether George Osborne's weakness is caused by his father's *nouveau riche* indulgence and whether Rawdon Crawley Junior will be brutalized by his mother's lack of love. At the same time he frets away at the possibility of an economic causation of personality. The nub of Thackeray's scepticism lies in the moment when Becky says to herself, 'I think I could be a good woman if I had five thousand a year', and in Thackeray's comment, 'And who knows but that Rebecca was right in her speculations'. *Vanity Fair* is the work of a moralist inquiring what kind of goodness it is that can be conditioned by five thousand a year.

Pursuing the metaphor of a sideshow at the Fair, Thackeray speaks of his people as puppets – the 'Becky Puppet' and 'the Amelia Doll'. That is not to imply they lack life of their own. The world has produced few books so utterly created, few assemblies of characters so completely self-propelled by great internal springs of the Life Force. The whole beauty of the book lies in the tension of applying the most rigorous conceivable analysis to an unfailing imaginative fertility – and only because the imagination and invention are unfailing can Thackeray in artistic terms afford and dare to press on to that ruthless point where nothing is left in the book that is sentimental or wishful. If the people are puppets, it is not Thackeray who is pulling the strings; he has pushed through all illusions to the disturbing and despairing speculation that human beings may be pulled by strings of circumstance, by the chances of upbringing and the mere accident of five thousand a year. And having brought us to this almost intolerable adult, unillusioned vision, this most sardonic of novelists compounds the exquisitely artistic pain he has inflicted on us by addressing us as children, and finishes his book: 'Ah! *Vanitas Vanitatum!* which of us is happy in this world? Which of us has his desire? or, having it, is satisfied? – Come, children, let us shut up the box and the puppets, for our play is played out.'

The Rights of Animals

Were it announced tomorrow that anyone who fancied it might, without risk of reprisals or recriminations, stand at a fourth-storey window, dangle out of it a length of string with a meal (labelled 'Free') on the end, wait till a chance passer-by took a bite and then, having entangled his cheek or gullet on a hook hidden in the food, haul him up to the fourth floor and there batter him to death with a knob-kerry, I do not think there would be many takers.

Most sane adults would, I imagine, sicken at the mere thought. Yet sane adults do the equivalent to fish every day: not in panic, sexual jealousy, ideological frenzy or even greed – many of our freshwater fish are virtually inedible, and not one of them constitutes a threat to the life, love or ideology of a human on the bank – but for amusement. Civilization is not outraged at their behaviour. On the contrary: that a person's hobby is fishing is often read as a guarantee of his sterling and innocent character.

The relationship of *homo sapiens* to the other animals is one of unremitting exploitation. We employ their work; we eat and wear them. We exploit them to serve our superstitions: whereas we used to sacrifice them to our gods and tear out their entrails in order to foresee the future, we now sacrifice them to Science and experiment on their entrails in the hope – or on the mere off-chance – that we might thereby see a little more clearly into the present. When we can think of no pretext for causing their death and no profit to turn it to, we often cause it none the less, wantonly, the only gain being a brief pleasure for ourselves, which is usually only marginally bigger than the pleasure we could have had without killing anything; we could quite well enjoy our marksmanship or cross-country galloping without requiring a real dead wild animal to shew for it at the end.

It is rare for us to leave wild animals alive; when we do, we often do not leave them wild. Some we put on display in a prison just large enough for them to survive, but not in any full sense to live, in. Others we trundle about the country in their prisons, pausing every now and then to put them on public exhibition performing, like clockwork, 'tricks' we have 'trained' into them. However, animals are not clockwork but instinctual beings. Circus 'tricks' are spectacular or risible as the case may be precisely *because* they violate the animals' instinctual nature – which is precisely why they ought to violate both our moral and our aesthetic sense.

But where animals are concerned humanity seems to have switched off its morals and aesthetics – indeed, its very imagination. Goodness knows, those facilities function erratically enough in our dealings with one another. But at least we recognize their faultiness. We spend an increasing number of our cooler moments trying to forestall the moral and aesthetic breakdowns which are liable, in a crisis, to precipitate us into atrocities against each other. We have bitter demarcation disputes about where the rights of one man end and those of the next man begin, but most men now acknowledge that there are such things as the rights of the next man. Only in relation to the next animal can civilized humans persuade themselves that they have absolute and arbitrary rights – that they may do anything whatever that they can get away with.

The reader will have guessed in some detail by now what sort of person he confronts in me: a sentimentalist; probably a killjoy; a person with no grasp on economic realities; a twee anthropomorphist, who attributes human feelings (and no doubt human names and clothes as well) to animals, and yet actually prefers animals to humans and would sooner succour a stray cat than an orphan child; a latter-day version of those folklore English spinsters who, in the nineteenth century, excited the ridicule of the natives by walking round Florence requesting them not to ill-treat their donkeys; and *par excellence*, of course, a crank.

Well. To take the last item first: if by 'crank' you mean 'abnormal', yes. My views are shared by only a smallish (but probably not so small as you think) part of the citizenry – as yet. Still, that proves nothing either way about the validity of our views. It is abnormal to be a lunatic convinced you are Napoleon, but equally (indeed, numerically considered, probably even more) abnormal to be a genius. The test of a view is its rationality, not the number of people who endorse it. It would have been cranky indeed in the ancient world to raise the question of the rights of slaves – so cranky that scarcely a voice went on record as doing so. To us it seems incredible that the Greek philosophers should have scanned so deep into right and wrong and yet never *noticed* the immorality of slavery. Perhaps three thousand years from now it will seem equally incredible that we do not notice the immorality of our oppression of animals.

Slavery was the ancient world's patch of moral and aesthetic insensitivity. Indeed, it was not until the eighteenth and nineteenth centuries of our own era that the human conscience was effectively and universally switched on in that respect. Even then, we went on with economic and social exploitations which stopped short of slavery only in constitutional status, and people were found to justify them. But by then the exploiters had at least been forced on to the defensive and felt obliged to produce the feeble arguments that had never even been called for in the ancient world. Perhaps it is a sign that our conscience is about to be switched on in relation to animals that some animal-exploiters are now seeking to justify themselves. When factory-farmers tell us that animals kept in 'intensive' (i.e. concentration) camps are being kindly spared the inclemency of a winter outdoors, and that calves do not mind being tethered for life on slate because they have never known anything else, an echo should start in our historical consciousness: do you remember how the childlike blackamoors were kindly spared the harsh responsibilities of freedom, how the skivvy didn't feel the hardship of scrubbing all day because she was used to it, how the poor didn't mind their slums because they had never known anything else?

The first of the factory-farmers' arguments is, of course, an argument for ordinary farms to make better provision for animals in winter, not for ordinary farms to be replaced by torture chambers. As for the one about the animals' never having known anything else, I still shan't believe it to be valid but I shall accept that the factory-farmers genuinely believe it themselves when they follow out its logic by using their profits to finance the repatriation of every circus and zoo animal that was caught in the wild, on the grounds that those *have* known something else.

Undismayed by being a crank, I will make you a free gift of another stick to beat me with, by informing you that I am a vegetarian. Now, surely, you have me. Not only am I a more extreme crank, a member of an even smaller minority, than you had realized; surely I *must*, now, be a killjoy. Yet which, in fact, kills more joy: the killjoy who would deprive you of your joy in eating steak, which is just one of the joys open to you, or the kill-animal who puts an end to all the animal's joys along with its life?

Beware, however (if we may now take up the first item in your Identikit portrait of me), how you call me a sentimentalist in this matter. I may be less of one than you are. I won't kill an animal in order to eat it, but I am no respecter of dead bodies as such. If our chemists discovered (as I'm sure they quickly would were there a demand) how to give tenderness and hygiene to the body of an animal which had died of old age, I would willingly eat it; and in principle that goes for human animals, too. In practice I suspect I should choke on a rissole which I knew might contain bits of Great-Aunt Emily (whether through love or repulsion I am not quite sure), and I admit I might have to leave rational cannibalism to future generations brought up without my irrational prejudice (which is equally irrational whether prompted by love or by repulsion). But you were accusing me, weren't you, of sentimentality and ignorance of economic realities. Have you thought how much of the world's potential food supply *you* unrealistically let go to waste because of your sentimental compunction about eating your fellow-citizens after they have lived out their natural lives?

If we are going to rear and kill animals for our food, I think we have a moral obligation to spare them pain and terror in both processes, simply because they are sentient. I can't *prove* they are sentient; but then I have no proof *you* are. Even though you are articulate, whereas an animal can only scream or struggle, I have no assurance that your 'It hurts' expresses anything like the intolerable sensations I experience in pain. I know, however, that when I visit my dentist and say 'It hurts', I am grateful that he gives me the benefit of the doubt.

I don't myself believe that, even when we fulfil our minimum obligation not to cause pain, we have the right to kill animals. I know I would have no right to kill you, however painlessly, just because I liked your flavour, and I am not in a position to judge that your life is worth more to you than the animal's to it. If anything, you probably value yours less; unlike the animal, you are capable of acting on an impulse to suicide. Christian tradition would permit me to kill the animal but not you, on the grounds that you have, and it hasn't, an immortal soul. I am not a Christian and do not avail myself of this licence; but if I were, I should in elementary justice see the soul theory as all the more reason to let the animal live out the one mortal life it has.

The only genuine moral problem is where there is a direct clash between an animal's life and a human one. Our diet proposes no such clash, meat not being essential to a human life; I have sustained a very healthy one for ten years without. And in fact such clashes are much rarer in reality than in exam papers, where we are always being asked to rescue either our grandmother or a Rubens from a blazing house. Human fantasy often fabricates a dilemma (yours did when you suggested I love animals in

127

preference to people – there is no psychological law which prevents me from loving both) as an excuse for inertia. It is a principle of 'divide and do nothing'. In reality, unless you truly send a cheque to a relief organization for humans, your preference for humans over animals does not justify you in resisting my hint that you should send one to the Wood Green Animal Shelters (601 Lordship Lane, London N22 5LG) and to Zoo Check, which was founded by Virginia McKenna and William Travers with the motto 'Keeping Wildlife in the Wild' (Cherry Tree Cottage, Coldharbour, Dorking, Surrey RH5 6HA).

The most seemingly genuine clash is on the subject of vivisection. To hold vivisection to be never justified is a hard belief. But so is its opposite. I believe it is never justified because I can see nothing (except our being able to get away with it) which lets us pick on animals that would not equally let us pick on idiot humans (who would be more useful) or, for the matter of that, on a few humans of any sort whom we might sacrifice for the good of the many. If we do permit vivisection, here if anywhere we are under the most stringent minimum obligations. The very least we must make sure of is that no experiment is ever duplicated, or careless, or done for mere teaching's sake or as a substitute for thinking. Knowing how often, in every other sphere, pseudo-work proliferates in order to fill time and jobs, and how often activity substitutes for thought, and then reading the official statistics about vivisection, do you truly believe we *do* make sure? (The National Anti-Vivisection Society is at 51 Harley Street, London W1.)

Our whole relation to animals is tinted by a fantasy – and a fallacy – about our toughness. We feel obliged to demonstrate we can take it; in fact, it is the animals who take it. So shy are we of seeming sentimental that we often disguise our humane impulses under 'realistic' arguments: foxhunting is snobbish; factory-farmed food doesn't taste so nice. But foxhunting would still be an atrocity if it were done by authenticated, pedigreed proletarians, and so would factory-farming, even if a way were found of making its corpses tasty. So, incidentally, would slavery, even if it were proved a hundred times more economically realistic than freedom.

The saddest and silliest of the superstitions to which we sacrifice animals is our belief that by killing them we ourselves somehow live more fully. We might live more fully by entering imaginatively into their lives. But shedding their blood makes us no more full-blooded. It is a mere myth, often connected with our myth about the *savoir vivre* and sexiness of the sunny south (which is how you managed to transform me into a frustrated British virgin in Florence). There is no law of nature which makes *savoir vivre* incompatible with 'live and let live'. The bullfighter who torments a bull to death and then castrates it of an ear has neither proved nor increased his own virility; he has merely demonstrated that he is a butcher with balletic tendencies.

Superstition and dread of sentimentality weight all our questions against the animals. We *don't* scrutinize vivisection rigorously – we somehow think it would be soft of us to do so, which we apparently think a worse thing to be than cruel. When, in February 1965, the House of Lords voted against a Bill banning animal acts from circuses, it was pointed out that the animal-trainers would lose their jobs. (Come to think of it, many human-trainers must have lost theirs when it was decided to ban gladiator acts from circuses.) No one pointed out how many unemployed acrobats and jugglers would *get* jobs to replace the animals. (I'm not, you see by the way, the sort of killjoy who wants to abolish the circus as such.) Similarly with the anthropomorphism argument, which works in both directions but is always wielded in one only. In the same House of Lords debate, Lady Summerskill, who had taken the humane side, was mocked by a noble lord on the grounds that were *she* shut up in a cage she would indeed suffer from mortification and the loss of her freedom, but an animal, not being human, wouldn't. Why did no one point out that a human, in such circumstances, dreadful as they are, would have every consolation of the human intellect and imagination, from reading books to analysing his circumstances and writing to the Home Secretary about them, whereas the animal suffers the raw terror of not comprehending what is being done to it?

In point of fact, I am the very opposite of an anthropomorphist. I don't hold animals superior or even equal to humans. The whole case for behaving decently to animals rests on the fact that we are the superior species. We are the species uniquely capable of imagination, rationality and moral choice – and that is precisely why we are under the obligation to recognize and respect the rights of animals.

In 1965 the *Sunday Times* invited me to write a full-page article on a subject of my choice. What I chose to write appears here without alteration (except that I have brought names and addresses up to date) and under the title it bore in the paper and in pamphlet form when it was reprinted by two organizations. Nowadays I should probably give it the title 'The Rights of the Other Animals', because much human oppression of animals of other species is masked by the arrogance with which humans forget that they are animals, too.

My first novel, which was my second fiction volume and which won first prize for a first novel at the Cheltenham Literary Festival, concerns the liberation of a large ape from London Zoo. It was first published in 1953 and has been more than once reprinted in paperback, though only fairly recently have I managed to secure a cover consisting of a detail from Stubbs's *Green Monkey* painting. In 1954 I became a vegetarian.

It was, however, the *Sunday Times* article of 1965 that made me a public exponent of the other animals' rights – a career that led me to many pleasures but also to nightmares and stage-fright. Virtually every book that was published on a subject related to those mentioned in my 'Rights of Animals' article was sent me by a literary editor for review. Descriptions or photographs from several haunted my mind in the way that earlier instances haunted, as he remarked in his writings, the mind of Bernard Shaw. I was attacked by stage-fright on the many occasions when I took part in discussions or debates on television, when I regularly feared (often, I suspect, correctly) that my facial fixity and my lack of fluency would harm rather than promote the case I was trying to present. The most terrifying stage-fright of my life gripped me until I began to speak (which for me has always at least half-melted the terror inseparable from public speaking) when I agreed to stand with the other speech-makers on the plinth of Nelson's Column in Trafalgar Square and thence address a Square- filling rally against factory-farming.

With unalloyed pleasure I made the acquaintance of, and often collaborated with, Richard D. Ryder, whose conscientiously researched and intellectually bold book *Victims of Science* has made him from 1975 onwards the leader of the movement for the rights of all animals in late-twentieth-century Britain. I also often worked with Muriel, the Lady Dowding, who, through Beauty Without Cruelty (Avebury Avenue, Tonbridge, Kent TN9 1TL), pioneered the now widely spread manufacture and international sale of scents, soaps and cosmetics without tests on or ingredients from non-human animals. I shared none of her supernatural beliefs but liked her tolerant and robust personality. I enjoyed visiting her at the architecturally handsome house she lived in during the sixties.

I became an anti-vivisectionist in 1954, largely because I find the arguments of Bernard Shaw (chiefly in the Preface to *The Doctor's Dilemma*) irrefutable. When I became a vegetarian in the same year I had never knowingly met a vegetarian of the human variety. Scrupulously I brought no emotional pressure (which the unscrupulous who use it prefer to call moral pressure, despite its patent immorality) to bear on Michael Levey, whom I married in 1954. Our daughter, Kate Levey, was born in 1957. I carefully did not bring her up on a vegetarian diet or propaganda. Independently, she became vegetarian when she was adolescent and has remained so ever since. Michael Levey, for reasons no less independent, became vegetarian (and a skilled vegetarian cook) soon after.

Moved by the distresses imposed on the beings from whom humans take milk and eggs, I became a vegan in 1980. Several interviewers have assumed that my vegetarianism or, as it now is, veganism must be adopted for the sake of my health. Not so. It is for the sake of the health of cows, bulls, sheep, hens, pigs, turkeys . . . Human beings, unlike cats, are physiologically equipped to be omnivorous. In diet they can without detriment to themselves do as imagination and conscience bid.

By chance as well as in my adventures in expounding the rights of the other animals I have now met many human vegetarians and vegans, of whom there are conscientiously estimated to be a million in Britain. That number makes it unsurprising that I have happened on many by chance. Towards increasing the total number, which must be done if oppression is to be removed, I am conscious that I am now not a good personal advertisement. In 1984 I lost the excellent health mentioned in my 1965 essay and was diagnosed as having multiple sclerosis. I remain vegan, of course. As a matter of fact, no one seriously suspects a connection with the illness, the cause of which is unknown to medical science.

The other pleasures I enjoyed as a result of writing the 1965 article were to meet several British academic philosophers who had taken up the same cause, to meet French vegetarian enthusiasts for the rights of the other animals and to make contact with an Italian group. With pleasure and pride I discovered that the first two paragraphs of my article were one of several inspirations in the foundation of the Campaign for the Abolition of Angling (PO Box 14, Romsey, SO5 9NN) and that its last sentence, 'freely translated into Italian', was cited in 1987 as a lecture-ending used by the head of the Cremona rescue and shelter unit of the Anglo-Italian Society for the Protection of Animals (136 Baker Street, London W1M 1FH).

Disablement by a disease that is a medical mystery further convinces me of the scientific ineptitude of seeking understanding by experiments on living beings of other-than-human species. The millions of pounds and dollars spent, and the millions of non-human lives and millions of human work-hours spent, have produced fewer valuable results than it is reasonable to expect from the investment. Of such results as there have been over decades no scientist can say with accuracy, though many scientists do say unscientifically, that the discoveries could not have been made by any other method. The crucial comparison is between the money, thought and work-hours spent on the other methods and those spent on the prestige-winning and fund-winning method of vivisection.

Vivisectors ignore the scientific fact that an animal, whether human or other-than-human by species, is an individual, an 'I'. Such ignoring of a cardinal fact relies on the fascist ethic that the strong need not concern themselves with the rights of those they can overcome. By its dependence on vivisection, medical science deprives itself of minds that refuse to shutter themselves behind practices and methods of testing hypotheses that have become routine. Medical, like other scientific, discovery will come from scientific intelligence exercised with flair. Minds capable of flair increasingly choose not to take up medical science as a result of its massive and unthinking routines of vivisection.

In the case of multiple sclerosis, no one has collected the statistics on which a scientific imagination might work. No one knows how many diagnosed cases there are in Britain or any other country. Figures cited are estimates. It is not possible to know accurately the geographical distribution of the illness, the proportion of men to women who have it, and how old they were when it was diagnosed.

The only investigation specifically into multiple sclerosis that undertakes not to use or fund vivisection is the Naomi Bransom Trust. Although the inquiry into the disease was active in 1988 at a British university, I could not find

133

an address for the Trust which it would be useful to cite. The Multiple Sclerosis Society is named among the many organizations that fund animal experimentation by the 11th Hour Group, which comprises scientists, nurses, doctors and patients who campaign against vivisection (326 Earlsfield Road, London SW18 3EJ). So does a group of patients under the name DAARE (Disabled Against Animal Research and Exploitation). DAARE's address is P.O. Box 8, Daventry, Northants NN11 4RQ. It promotes and publicizes humane methods of discovering facts and proposing and testing remedies.

Goldfinch by Carel Fabritius

The small painting of a goldfinch by Carel Fabritius is one of the world's memorable pictures: simple in the extreme and yet deeply enigmatic.

The goldfinch, who is an adult male, stands with his body in profile to the spectator, but he has turned his head and is looking out of the picture virtually front-face.

Is the picture a portrait? The question, to which I think the answer is almost certainly 'Yes', is no whimsy. I was for some years on terms of talk-and-touch friendship with several wild and free urban pigeons. I learned what I imagine better-versed humans have always known: out of dozens of the same species you recognize the birds you are acquainted with exactly as you recognize your human acquaintances in a crowded room – by the individual cast of their faces.

Even had the subject's identity become lost, a painting of an adult male human isolated in a comparable pose would be acknowledged as, specifically, a portrait. Indeed, the National Gallery in London houses just such a portrait, by Titian, of a now unknown man. Titian deploys a pose not unlike that of the goldfinch painted by Fabritius to display both the individual face and a human equivalent of plumage, the man's sumptuous and quilted blue sleeve.

About the status of the bird that Fabritius depicted there is no puzzle. He is a captive and a slave. Probably some human claims to own him.

He stands on a small (scarcely taller that he) wall-mounted structure that resembles a tiny writing desk and that is half-girdled by two curved wooden fenders. He has put his foot on the upper fender. A chain is attached to his leg. The other end of the chain finishes in a ring which has been secured by being slipped round the fender. The brief slack middle of the chain hangs down in a loop.

The goldfinch is doomed to continual frustration of his instinctual activities including the activity to which instinct prompts such birds the moment they can do it well enough to quit the nest. Whether he tries a short arc or a direct line, the goldfinch can fly only so far as the tether permits. When he reaches the limit he will be tugged back in mid-flight. For perch he has choice only of the main structure up against the wall or the not distant fenders. He cannot act even on his instinct to seek food and drink. They are provided. Water, I surmise, is in the inkwell-shaped vessel at the left on the main perch, to which it imparts the look of a desk for a left-handed human.

It is clear from portraits that it was not uncommon in seventeenth-century Europe for a slave bird to be handed over to a human child, whose inquisitive fingers must have increased the bird's distresses and who used the bird as an animate, perpetually mobile, toy. If the parents had the requisite money and pride of family, child and slave bird were sometimes portrayed together. I imagine that to have a 'toy' in hand was meant to induce the child to keep still while the painter took the likeness.

Even so, the treatment to which the child subjects the bird in paintings is often boisterous. Finches of all kinds are associated with, and were evidently thought appropriate for, little boys and not little girls. The free end of the bird's tether might be held or attached to a stick that was held by the boy, and the bird, who no doubt *tried* to fly, was thus transformed into a kind of whirligig.

If Fabritius's painting of the goldfinch truly is a portrait, it may be, so to speak, a double portrait, of boy plus bird, from which the boy has been left out.

That notion might make it less surprising than you might otherwise consider it that, at a time when it was not the standard practice it became in the nineteenth and twentieth centuries for painters to sign and date their works, the painting bears near the bottom edge of the paint surface the inscription 'C. Fabritius 1654'.

The inscription relieves art-historians of their customary problems, to attribute the picture to a painter and to place it chronologically in his oeuvre. The year 1654 was in fact that of Fabritius's untimely death in the explosion of the arsenal at Delft. The inscription may, however, answer the usual questions only to pose others.

The name is not in signature form or even abbreviated into a monogram. It is in bold, highly legible, capital letters.

The painted goldfinch above it is about the size of a goldfinch in real life. Indeed, the picture is often described as belonging to the genre which the English language, with its habit of half-eating fragments of other languages like lumps of chewing gum, calls '*trompe l'œil*'.

The eye that such paintings were primarily designed to deceive was, of course, a human one. Yet there is an anecdote from the ancient world about the most famous of ancient Greek painters, Apelles, in which the eye that was deceived by a painting of an animal was an animal's eye.

No work by Apelles survived into the modern world. What made him the Renaissance's best-known ancient Greek painter was chiefly the collection by ancient Romans, and the recounting in Latin, of anecdotes about him, together with his being the favourite painter of Alexander the Great, who would, indeed, have his portrait painted by no one else.

Apelles was renowned for the verisimilitude of his work. He seems to have shared Alexander's gift of uniting popular and learned taste in his praise, and it is verisimilitude, no doubt the point on which the union was gathered, that the anecdotes emphasize.

In one such anecdote Apelles paints Alexander in company with a horse. He shows the painting to Alexander, who, unusually, expresses dissatisfaction. While the painting is on display, a less famous horse than Alexander's mount, Bucephalus, chances to pass, spots the painted horse and neighs in greeting. The master of painting tells the master of much of the known world that the passing horse has demonstrated better artistic taste than he.

Such was the Renaissance respect for, and emulation of, classical precedent that modern-world painters incorporated an imagined Apelles in their 'history' paintings and their biographers recast many of the stories recorded of him. Several latter-day painters were credited with a verisimilitude that deceived the eyes of diverse animals into mistaking a painted animal or fruit for the real thing.

In the spirit of the anecdote about Apelles and the passing horse or of one of its many modern-world variants, Fabritius designed his goldfinch painting, I conjecture, to deceive a goldfinch – the very one whose portrait I conceive it to be.

In the twentieth century humans still enslave birds. The massive enslavement is of birds whom the slave-owners intend to kill in order to sell their corpses for humans to eat. Less often, smaller birds are enslaved and sold to give emotional rather than gastronomic-plus-emotional pleasure to humans who keep them captive – if not on chains, then in cages – to delight the 'owners' by their prettiness. Animal captives, humans included, are liable to boredom. To the human gaoler of a small caged bird it seems a natural act of kindness to seek to relieve the boredom of the bird, whom the human is using as an emotional toy, by providing toys for the bird. The toy most commonly put inside the cage of a small slave bird is a mirror. The slave-owners are amused by his antics if the bird is tempted into curiosity or even courtship by his own simulacrum.

The real-life solitary captive goldfinch, chained to a perch up against the inside wall of a room, was, I think, meant to be briefly diverted when he turned his head, looked across the room and saw a painted simulacrum of himself doing exactly the same on a matching perch on the wall opposite.

The light-coloured background of the painting gives the impression that the perch is fixed to a painted and plastered internal wall and the bird to the perch. However, the curved fenders join the wall without visible fastening. The ends of the fenders must slide into holes in the wall, and that would make it easy, as indeed it had to be, to pull out one end and slip the ring securing the bird on and off.

So simple and efficient a device would not, I think, be practical in a plaster wall, which would crumble if holes were introduced into it and frequently used. I conceive that the internal walls of the room were in fact panelled in wood. To one the perch for the real goldfinch was fixed. On the opposite wall the simulacrum was painted directly on the wood.

The painting is indeed on panel – described as 'unusually thick' in Christopher Brown's 1981 volume on the painter (to which I am in debt for the documented facts about Fabritius's life and works).

The shadows in the painting are no doubt plausibly disposed in relation to a real light-source, probably a window, in the room. The painting is given its light background in order to shew up the shadows and the coloration of the painted bird. Perhaps the wood behind the real-life bird was also painted in order to shew *him* up.

If the painting was done on a flat, oblong section of the wood panelling, then the raised and perhaps carved sections surrounding it would automatically provide the painting with a wooden frame in the natural colour of the wood.

After Fabritius's sudden accidental death, the picture, as a potentially valuable and saleable object, was, I think, cut out of the wood panelling in order to render it portable. The nail-holes which X-ray discloses along the edges of the panel but which X-ray cannot date are probably, though unprovably, the result of some subsequent owner's fixing the now portable picture in something resembling what he was told was its original site.

To paint a portrait of a goldfinch on part of a panelled room is something Fabritius might have done virtually anywhere to commission. Evidently he executed some such commission (or kindness) in Delft; in a contract of 1660 a widow sold a brewery there with the stipulation that she be allowed to remove a painting by Carel Fabritius that

was very firmly attached to one of the inside walls, provided she made good any damage the removal caused.

All the same, the inscription painted on it convinces me
that it was on a panel in a panelled room in his own house
that Fabritius painted his goldfinch picture – and with
specific purpose.

Fabritius (or Fabricius) was the surname taken by the
painter's father in imitation of a Latin *nomen*. The *nomen*
which, when it belonged to a man, always ended in *-ius*,
was the middle component of a tripartite ancient Roman
name or the second when there were only two parts, which
there were when the bearer did not belong to a noble
family. The *-ius* ending is the masculine adjectival form
derived from the name of the *gens*, the clan, of the person
who bore the name.

Fabritius's father designed himself a name in Latinate
form by making an *-ius* adjective from the common Latin
noun *faber*, a word often translatable into English as
'carpenter' but often assuming other meanings, from arti-
san to minor engineer.

The Latin essence is to convey dexterity and ingenuity
in practical constructions.

Most of the meanings the Latinate name can bear seem
to have been practised by Carel Fabritius as ways of earning a living. He is recorded as having been a carpenter,
which may have meant a deviser and builder of various
constructions; and at least one of his paintings demonstrates he combined his skill as an illusionist painter
with his skill at designing and making practical (in the
sense that they would work) objects.

I conceive that he made the real perch and that he
designed and probably executed the easily moved means
whereby its fenders entered the wood-clad wall.

He acquired the real-life slave goldfinch, installed him
in the Fabritius house and painted his likeness opposite
him for the amusement and instruction, I believe, of a
small boy.

No candidate is recorded from the painter's own two
marriages. However, Carel Fabritius became in 1651 one

of two legal guardians of two orphaned boys. The younger, a child of the right sex to play with a captive finch, was, in 1654 (the year of the inscription) aged about nine. (He was four when his father died in 1649.)

I think it likely that in 1654 Carel Fabritius began to exercise a guardian's responsibilities by arranging for the boy to visit the Fabritius home regularly and there undertake a course of lessons, possibly administered and very probably drawn up by Carel Fabritius himself, to whom, as the son of a professional schoolmaster, such a procedure cannot have been alien.

After his lessons the boy was to be rewarded by a romp with the real-life goldfinch. During lessons the image of the bird was to promise him later reward; and the inscription it surmounted was, I conceive, what teachers nowadays call a 'visual aid', a mixture of wall chart and permanent entry on a blackboard.

The date familiarized the pupil with the Arabic numerals and the dating system used in modern-world western Europe. The figures were able to do service in mental arithmetic; and since the year was that when the instruction began it was an encouraging means for noting the pupil's progress.

The letters, besides making the boy familiar with the name of one of his two guardians, were serviceable in teaching Latin. 'Fabritius' could be used as an instance of a second-declension masculine singular adjective or noun and the boy required to write or recite the paradigm of its inflexions. 'C. Fabritius' was at the same time an example of the ancient Roman system of names, in which the first component was abbreviated to an initial or pair of them. The *C* would have stood in a Roman name for Gaius (or in its alternative spelling Caius).

The script of the capital letters further provided instruction and practice in reading Latin inscriptions cut, whether in the ancient or in the modern world, in stone – on, for instance, monuments or buildings. As though in such an inscription, the capital *U* of Fabritius has the shape of a *V*.

Masterly painter, schoolmaster, abused bird and instructed boy are all dead. The image abides, posing mechanistic puzzles, which one can try to answer by logical conjecture, and presenting the insoluble and almost unbearable enigma of the existence, once, of a captive bird and the existence, now, of the image of the bird looking out from the picture that imprisons it.

Felines

I know of only one historical hypothesis that is instantly convincing. I read it in the Autumn 1985 number of *The Ashmolean*, a lively and scholarly quarterly with subjects as various as the collections in the museum that issues it. An article explored ancient Egyptian representations, including some piercingly beautiful statuettes, of cats: plumpish, sleek and palpably domestic. It recorded the arrival of domestic cats in Europe from Egypt, sketched the theological context in which ancient Egyptian culture set them and traced their probable evolution from two or more species of wild small cat found in North Africa. Wild cats, the article suggested, made their own way into human settlements. Because they killed mice, rats and snakes, the humans did not discourage them. Thus it came about that, alone of non-human animals, 'the cat may have domesticated itself'.

That process the hero of *Stray* reverses – and with just cause. From the probable bargain struck in outposts of ancient Egypt it is the humans who are the defaulters. A. N. Wilson details their treachery here and now, in Britain or in whichever other English-speaking, technology-idolatrous society you care to take for the background of his new novel. The narrative is the oral autobiography of an ageing, seven-year-old alley-cat ('an "alley- cat" is what I am and proud of it'), told to one of his countless grandsons, most of whom he does not know or want to. He becomes a voluntary stray. He lives out of dustbins, by hunting and by filching the food put out for stay-at-home cats. He joins a 'commune' of strays. The whole group is captured by humans and sold to a vivisection laboratory. The horror of that part of the narrative is that none of it is invented.

Betrayed and tortured by humans, the alley-cat is scrupulous in his assessment of them. It is liberationist humans, brave enough to break the law, who bring about his escape from the laboratory. He praises the 'good woman' in whose home he and his brother grow up, though he condemns her and other carnivorous humans' hypocrisy when she is displeased with the cats' proud gifts to her of the corpses of birds they have killed. He commends human ingenuity in keeping corpses fresh in cans. He admires the wit of a nun who makes the stray acceptable to a nunnery by letting him pass for female. Perhaps the other nuns belong to the large group of English-speakers that defies biology by assuming that all cats are female and all dogs male.

The better-informed nun remarks that the stray's ancestors were worshipped in ancient Egypt, and there are unemphasized traces of Egypt strewn through the book. The commune's boss, tragically unable to protect his underlings, insists on being called 'Tom-Cat' despite the narrator's explanation that that is merely the generic name by which humans describe male cats. Perhaps he is modelling himself on the 'Great Tom Cat' whom, according to the *Ashmolean* article, Egyptians considered a manifestation of the sun-god. The narrator calls the moon 'our great Mother-of-Night', a title that perhaps remembers Isis, perhaps via *The Magic Flute*.

Keeping in touch with one's children and grandchildren the alley-cat considers to be a habit of humans, and one that occasions them unhappiness or, at the least, pretence. Towards love he has long held the traditional attitude towards heterosexuality of humans educated at British public schools: that it will arrive, but later. Only his late-arrived love for a female cat prompts him to an interest in, and a visit to, her and the kittens she bears in the 'heiring cupboard' of a human household. His unprecedented narration to his grandson is designed to teach him that he is 'a cat and not a slave to any other creature in the universe' and to forewarn him that cats' experience is chiefly of 'unending and unexplained loss'.

Loss is for the most part occasioned by humans, who claim to 'own' cats with power over them of life and death, ease and agony. Perceiving results and not motives, the alley-cat no more conceives of accidental or natural death than he at first did of love. Cars are to him 'engines of murder'.

To the hero-narrator of *Stray* all humans are evil-smelling. In real life I suspect that cats, though themselves predators to their very bellies, which cannot be adequately nourished on vegetable food, do not dislike the smell of non-carnivorous humans, who presumably do not seem rival and larger predators.

Since many cats help themselves occasionally to vegetables, an ingenious and human chemist would do universal good were he to find a way of making vegetarian food adequate to cats so that a human who nurtures a cat in hearth and heart need not be the effective murderer of animals of other species.

A. N. Wilson has written a classic in the sense that *Black Beauty* is a classic. His narrative technique is, however, appropriate for the age of the 1980s. What age of reader, in the sense of *aetatis suae*, he would consider ideal I cannot guess and it does not much matter. He is apprehensible to anyone literate. His episodic, quasi-picaresque (no rogue, his hero is the most honourable personality the reader meets) story is deeply read-on, funny, moving and exciting. He has devised a largely unlocated idiom that does plausible service for the language a cat might acquire from human associates. Cats' jokes, as unmistakable as cats' play (which rests on fantasy), transpose excellently into the narrative's puns.

A. N. Wilson joins the honourable list of established novelists, a list that includes Richard Adams, who have risked their status by using their skill and, most notably, their imagination in order to exercise the imagination of readers on behalf of animals of other species. May he summon them to protest as well as to provide sanctuary. The biographical note that accompanies the volume quotes his statement that the book will have been 'well

worth writing' if reading it 'prevents one adult from tortur-
ing a cat in a laboratory, or one child from tormenting a
cat in a backyard, or one family from getting a kitten when
they have no idea how to provide for its needs'.

C.H.A.T. (Celia Hammond Animal Trust, Wadhurst, East
Sussex TN5 6LB) re-homes animals who have been
abandoned by humans. By neutering, it aims to reduce the
population of strays on which human torturers prey.

The November-December 1988 issue of *The Vegetarian*
(Vegetarian Society UK, Parkdale, Dunham Road,
Altrincham, Cheshire WA14 4QG) reviewed *Dogs and
Cats Go Vegetarian* by B. L. Peden, which claims that
cats can be healthy vegetarians with the help of a diet
supplement. In the USA the publishers are Harbingers of
a New Age. In Britain both the book and Vegecat Sup-
plement are distributed by Hampshire Wholefoods, The
Black Horse, Winchester Road, Shedfield, Southampton
SO3 2HS.

Felines in Verse

Cats' Parnassus consists of six brief poems by John Heath-Stubbs. The language is easy to understand and the rhythms easily echo in the memory. Yet both are so dexterously wielded that the effect, like that of much of the domestic architecture of the eighteenth century, is of elegance. Not without reason does the first poem commemorate the cat with whom Dr Johnson chose to share 'His plain commodious mansion in Gough Square'.

In the affectionately symbiotic relationships here recreated, it is the humans who, as famous writers of English, have scaled Parnassus. Jeoffry (spelling blessed by humans who, even if clinically sane, are confused by the two orthodox spellings of Geoffrey/Jeffrey) laments the suffering of Christopher Smart. Selima, whose stressed first syllable suggests that hers was a feminine version of the name of the Pasha in *Die Entführung*, undergoes the same horrific death as she does in Gray's *other* elegy. She drowns again in the identical rhyme (side/dyed) and for the same cause: despite their fellow-feeling with humans, cats will not let their smaller and more edible fellow-animals, such as fish and birds, live. The cat who is Matthew Arnold's companion gluttonously covets his other companion. The poem might borrow the name of that often re-made comedy-thriller of the cinema, *The Cat and the Canary*.

Several of the cats call their human companion 'my master'. The locution marks the essential politeness many cats manifest towards humans. It is no more to be taken literally than the 'my mistress' of an Elizabethan sonnet.

Proceeding more by allusion than by parody, the poems observe feline and egalitarian courtesy towards both their

153

themes and their readers. The limerick that celebrates Edward Lear follows the form Lear established, repeating the rhyme-word of its first line in that of it last. Out of this pamphlet, where each poem faces a black-and-white illustration, the reader could quarry a literary quiz to which the text of the poems, with one exception, provides the answers. Only the poem where an anonymous cat visits T. S. Eliot neglects the name Eliot. Perhaps Mr Heath-Stubbs finally despaired when he conceived a reader whose ear could not tell him why, while the visiting cat curls up in Eliot's abode, 'The alley strays are caterwauling / Around St Stephen's Gloucester Road'. Or was it the result of a sudden fear that the cats had eaten the nightingales who had been singing near?

Sentimentality
and Louisa M. Alcott

Who's afraid of Louisa M. Alcott? Well, I for one and, for another, Louisa M. Alcott.

I'm afraid of her in a quite straightforward way – because she makes me cry. Being myself an almost wholly unsentimental writer, I'm not a bit afraid of her example, which doesn't tempt me. It's not as a writer but as a reader that I fear her.

Her own fear of herself was, however, more ambiguous. She is, I suppose, of all writers the one whose name *means* sentimentality: and yet sentimentality is what she and her characters most dread. Indeed, the very reason why Josephine March preferred to be known as Jo (and I would guess the nickname was the final simple stroke which turned her into one of the classic characters of popular-cum-nursery culture, up there with Sherlock Holmes and Little Miss Muffet) is that she found the name Josephine 'so sentimental'.

I was driven back to Louisa M. Alcott, whom I hadn't read since I was fourteen, by the 1964 revival on television of the old film of *Little Women*. By the 'old film' I mean the one with the young Katharine Hepburn – and there I instantly caution myself not to render unto Alcott credit which belongs to Hepburn. The cinematic personality of Katharine Hepburn (for which I imagine the credit belongs to the real-life personality of Katharine Hepburn) is one of those purely poetic literary inventions like Rosalind or the very idea of a seraph. Tears shed over Hepburn are diamonds, cutting clean and deep lacerations into the cheeks they course down. They have no connexion at all with the synthetically pearled snail-track left by the tears of sentimentality. It was just Louisa M. Alcott's good posthumous luck that Hepburn played Jo and that the high ruffled necks of 'period' clothes (to use the word in its purely evocative or estate agent's sense) set off to perfection the essentially tragic sinewiness of the Hepburn throat.

And yet: one can't say Alcott did nothing to deserve her luck. Hepburn was never so ideally cast again. It's already something that Alcott created the character which most perfectly became her. And then – the clinching point – the film provoked tears even when Hepburn was not on the screen.

It also brought back enough memory of the text for me to think that it was sticking fairly reverently to Alcott situations and dialogue – which I soon afterwards confirmed by getting hold of the book or, rather, books; the film is in fact taken from both *Little Women* and *Good Wives*. Buying them turned out to be an exercise in itself in nostalgia for a pre-war childhood. They were pretty well the last genuine *books*, with binding and dust wrapper, to be had for a paperback price. Presumably, therefore, they still sold in the 1960s, in commercially worthwhile quantities (though as they are out of copyright there is no author's royalty to add its mite to the selling price). Indeed, perhaps they still sold as a going contemporary concern: for though the publishers admit, by the clothes on the pictorial wrappers, that the stories themselves are 'period', there is nothing to make it unequivocally clear that they weren't written yesterday. You have to consult a reference book to discover that *Little Women* was first published in 1868. The blurb of one edition still speaks of 'Miss Alcott' – which seems to surrender the advantages of suggesting she's immortal in favour of those of suggesting she's still alive.

Having re-read them, dried my eyes and blown my nose (it is itself a sentimentality that this less dignified aspect of weeping is so seldom mentioned: one day I shall go through the fiction in the public library and to every 'His eyes filled' add 'so did his nose'), I resolved that the only honourable course was to come out into the open and admit that the dreadful books are masterpieces. I do it, however, with some bad temper and hundreds of reservations.

For, of course, to admit sentimentality at all is to play with fire. Sentimentality is always doing something of which art can stand only very small and controlled amounts – bursting out of the conventions of art and making a direct appeal (all art makes an oblique one) to real life. Sentimentality is always playing on your experience of real drowned kittens and real lost mothers – or, worse still, playing on your real dread of losing kittens or mothers. The weepiest of trashy movies is the one which throws in a moment or two of genuine newsreel. And then, having invoked the reality of the real world, sentimentality does the one thing neither morality nor art can stand for – it is hypocritical.

The true artistic impulse is, largely, cruel – or at least relentless. To bring a novel, for instance, to a climax, the artist must drive the situation, and probably the characters, to extremes. He harries his *donnée* until it falls apart and its logical structure is pitilessly exposed. The sentimentalist, on the other hand, is a non-artist, who won't take the responsibility of being ruthless. He won't drive his situations to the point of artistic inevitability. Instead, he appears to hold his hand in compunction. He resigns himself – much too soon – to the will of God; but covertly he is manipulating the will of God to suit what he is too hypocritical to admit is really his own taste.

Hundreds of fictional infants were, so to speak, raped on their deathbeds by Victorian anecdotalists – both novelists and painters – in order to procure for author and audience the pleasure of destroying an innocence but in such a way that the pleasure could pass for the quite innocent, even creditable, enjoyment of feeling a spasm across the eyelids. Even now one cannot stand quite indifferent beside those deathbeds. I think Oscar Wilde said that no man of feeling could read the death of Little Nell without laughing. But the unwitty and much more terrible truth is that no one can read it without crying. Dickens has made the illegitimate appeal to real life and, no matter what ludicrous nonsense he makes of the death of Little Nell, the death of children *is* sad.

The sentimentalist always breaks the rules of art and frequently those of morality. The most unforgivable of all the occasions when sentimentality has burst through the artistic conventions is the one when Peter Pan bursts through the proscenium and invites the audience to keep Tinker Bell alive by affirming that they believe in fairies. That the audience consists of children is the ultimate sentimental immorality. Christendom's inveterate habit of telling its children fairy-tales and then breaking the convention by assuring them that the tale is true and they must feel obliged to its hero, who died for *them*, is, though not justified, mitigated by the fact that most of the adults concerned really believe the story themselves and certainly believe it would do the children good to believe it. But I will not accept for a moment that J. M. Barrie had any more belief in fairies than – well, than the children in his audiences had.

When Theseus calls the lovers' account of what took place in that wood near Athens 'antique fables' and 'fairy toys', Hippolyta objects that their story 'More witnesseth than fancy's images, / And grows to something of great constancy.' So it does: to a fairy-tale genuinely imagined (and therefore genuinely and poetically moving), which is to be believed utterly – but strictly in the realm of the imagination. But Peter Pan's telling the audience that Tinker Bell 'thinks she could get well again if the children believed in fairies . . . If you believe, clap your hands!' is moral torture inflicted by a wanton – but masterly – sentimentalist. Ours is a paradoxical society, which dreads that one of its children might come on that charming, sentimentality-free little tale *Fanny Hill* and yet for decades put on *Peter Pan* at the very times of day and year when it was most likely to be seen by children. (Unless our winter holiday is in fact built round not the 25th December but the 28th – which commemorates the Slaughter of the Innocents?)

I have never supported censorship, even for *Peter Pan*.

I think society would be wise to treat *Peter Pan* as a play for adults, as we already sensibly do its runners-up as sentimental masterpieces for the theatre, *Private Lives* and *Who's Afraid of Virginia Woolf?*

It would certainly be unkind to deprive adults of *Peter Pan*, because as a piece of craftsmanship it is perhaps the most highly skilled job in the repertory, and is therefore capable of giving pleasure to two groups which more usually fail to agree on anything. For, incongruously enough, it is on works of literary craftsmanship that highbrow and lowbrow can often meet. Really, of course, they are at cross purposes. The lowbrow cares nothing for technique, and probably doesn't even notice it as such. All he wants is a good read at or a good cry over a good story; and he wants to have that without subjecting himself to the subversive effect – whether of society or of individual emotions – which is inherent in all good works of art. The highbrow, on the other hand, studies technique in order to pick up tips, which he intends to put to use in better appreciating, or even better practising, the subversiveness of art. But though they are at cross purposes and the lowbrow wouldn't approve of the highbrow's purpose if he knew of it, both highbrow and lowbrow (the two cultures which our apparently single culture is divided into) are glad, through simple good will, of any meeting place. They could go further and find worse rendezvous than Louisa M. Alcott.

You can measure Louisa Alcott's technical skill by asking any professional novelist how he would care to have to differentiate the characters of four adolescent girls – particularly if he were confined to a domestic setting, more-or-less naturalism and the things which were mentionable when Alcott wrote. Alcott triumphed at the technical problem, incidentally turning out for one of her four, Meg, a brilliant portrait of the sort of girl whose character consists of having no character. Girls of this sort are the commonest to meet in life and the rarest in literature, because they are so hard to depict (the problem is a variant of the old one about depicting a bore without being boring): usually it takes the genius of a Tolstoy (who specialized in them) to bring them off.

Whereas Meg was a commonplace of Alcott's own – or any – time, in Amy, Louisa Alcott shewed sociological prescience. Or, rather, I think, it shewed despite her. Try as she will to prettify and moralize, she cannot help making Amy the prototype of a model which did not become numerous in the United States until the twentieth century – the peroxided, girl-doll gold-digger. *Of course* it's Amy who gets Laurie in the end (he's rich, isn't he?): she's had 'Good pull-in for Laurie' emblazoned on her chest from the moment it began to bud.

With Beth, I admit, Alcott went altogether too far. Beth's patience, humility and gentle sunniness are a quite monstrous imposition on the rest of the family – especially when you consider at what close, even cramped, quarters they live (two bedrooms to four girls): no one in the household could escape the blight of feeding unworthy which was imposed by Beth. I concur in the judgment of the person with whom I watched the film (and who wept even more than I did) in naming her 'the Black Beth'. (I also concur in his naming Marmee 'Smarmee'.)

I think Louisa Alcott may herself have had an inkling that in designing a fate for Beth she was inspired by revenge. She seems, perhaps through suspicion of her own motives, to have faltered, with the result that she committed the sort of blunder only a very naïve technician would fall into and only a very self-assured one could, as she does, step out of in her stride. She brings Beth to the point of dying in *Little Women*, and then lets her recover; whereupon, instead of washing her hands – as not ruthless enough to do it – of the whole enterprise, she whips the situation up again in *Good Wives* and this time does ('As Beth had hoped, "the tide went out easily"') kill her off.

As for Laurie: well, of course, Laurie is awful, tossing those awful curls (though in *Good Wives* he has them cropped and is told off for it): yet though I will go to my death (may the tide go out easily) denying that Laurie has a millionth part of the attraction Louisa Alcott thinks he has and the girls think he has, I cannot deny that he is lifelike. If you want to see the romanticized implausibility which even an intelligent woman of the world (and great novelist into the bargain) could make of a curly-haired young man, look at George Eliot's Will Ladislaw. Laurie by contrast is – if awfully – probable.

In the most important event affecting Laurie, the fact that Jo refuses him, Alcott goes beyond verisimilitude and almost into artistic honesty. No doubt she found the courage for this, which meant cutting across the cliché-lines of the popular novel and defying her readers' matchmaking hopes, in the personality of Jo. Jo is one of the most blatantly autobiographical yet most fairly treated heroines in print. All that stands between her and Emma Woodhouse is her creator's lack of intellect. Alcott is not up to devising situations which analyse and develop, as distinct from merely illustrating, her characters.

And in fact absence of intellectual content is the mark of the sentimental genre; conversely, it is because of her intellect that Jane Austen is never sentimental. I think, incidentally, that the word 'sentimental' may have been in bad repute with Louisa Alcott because in 1868 it still wore eighteenth-century dress. And the reason, of course, why the eighteenth-century sentimental mode, unlike the nineteenth-century one, no longer works on us (the death of Virginie in *Paul et Virginie* really can't be read without laughing) is that the eighteenth century was so double-dyed intellectual that it *couldn't* put aside intellect when it took out its handkerchief: its many attempts to be affectingly simple were made self-conscious and absurd by its (perfectly correct) suspicion that it was being a simpleton.

As sentimentalists go, Louisa M. Alcott is of the gentler and less immoral sort. Beth's is the only really lushed-over death (the canary who dies in Chapter Eleven of *Little Women* is virtually a throw-away): on the whole, Alcott prefers to wreak her revenges on her characters by making them unhappy in their moments of happiness. (They make it easy for her to do so, through their own proneness to

163

sentimentality.) Even here, one can morally if not aesthetically justify her. It's all, so to speak, between consent-
ing adolescents. All four girls are quite masochists enough
to enjoy what she does to them.

I rest on Louisa M. Alcott my plea – hedged about with
provisos, reduced, indeed, to a mere strangled sob – that
we should recognize that, though sentimentality mars art,
craftsmanship in sentimentality is to be as legitimately
enjoyed as in any of those genres (thrillers, pornography,
ghost stories, yarns, science fiction – whichever way your
taste lies) which, because they suppress some relevant
strand in artistic logic, are a little less than literature. The
spasm across the eyelids is not inherently more despicable
than the frisson of the supernatural or the muted erotic
thrill imparted by a brilliant sado-erotic literary craftsman
like Raymond Chandler. It is, however, more dangerous.
I wish its imagery were more vegetarian but I think one
should take to heart this stray little fable by Kierkegaard
(whose personality is, indeed, to be taken to heart in all
contexts): 'In itself, salmon is a great delicacy; but too
much of it is harmful, since it taxes the digestion. At one
time when a very large catch of salmon had been brought
to Hamburg, the police ordered that a householder
should give his servants only one meal a week of salmon.
One could wish for a similar police order against
sentimentality.'

Ellen Terry

The letters of Ellen Terry, her 1987 biographer says, 'bring us as close as we can come to the actress's own voice'. That is not so, marvellous though many of her letters are. By discontinuing the machines and styluses that play 78 rpm discs, capitalism has plunged Britain into much the condition of the island in *The Tempest* before the first human incursion. Dozens of spirits are imprisoned in trees or at least in record cabinets. I do not suppose I am the only person with a copy of HMV's single-sided disc numbered 2-3535 even though, without the help of some Prospero, I can no longer release its soundtrack – which is Ellen Terry's recitation of Portia's 'The quality of mercy' speech.

Her speaking voice is of middle pitch. Her accent is 'standard English'. She speaks fast but her articulation crisply separates word from word. Bernard Shaw, whose own excellent articulation served him well in public speaking, described Ellen Terry's as 'perfect' and likened her to Queen Victoria, 'one of the most perfect speakers of her day'.

The new biography does not know that its subject's voice is recorded, though a 'Chronology' at the back logs, under 1916–22, her appearance in 'five forgettable films'. From the dates I assume they are silent. As a matter of fact, Shaw met her by chance 'in the country near Elstree' while one of her films was shot. He describes the meeting ('She was astonishingly beautiful') in his Preface to their published correspondence.

As he points out there, she was never stage-struck. Children of travelling actors, she and her elder sister, Kate, who also became a star, were born into their profession.

Ellen's literal birth was in lodgings at Coventry in, she and Shaw believed, 1848. After her death Roger Manvell established that her true year of birth was 1847. She was always a year older than she thought, said and wrote that she was. It is one of the rare points where her autobiography cannot steer a later biographer. Professor Auerbach fills in with a conjecture that her father made a deliberate mistake in order to smooth her transition from juvenile trouser rôles to womanly rôles. How early in her babyhood he foresaw the need and whether he did the same kindness for his elder daughter with the result that Kate Terry's date of birth is erroneous, too, the conjecture does not explore.

Earning her own living from childhood and free from the hypocrisies of dependence, Ellen Terry became one of the least Victorian of Victorians. She left the theatre without rue when, in 1864, she married her senior by thirty years, the painter and sculptor George Frederick Watts (whose middle name the 1987 biography of Ellen Terry docks of the final *k* many authorities accord it). The paintings for which she sat, to him made her 'interesting and singular' being known to Shaw before he arrived in London and saw her on the stage. Yet within a year of the marriage Watts returned her like an unsatisfactory mail order. She went briefly back to the theatre but quit it again when she set up house with the architect and designer E. W. Godwin, to whom she bore her two children, Edith and Gordon. The household split apart. She resumed acting, secured divorce from Watts and married the man who played Benedick to her first Beatrice. He meant to give his surname to her children, but Craig, the surname under which they as adults acted, produced and wrote, was appropriated, by Edith, from a Scottish landmark. Ellen Terry became the regular co-star of Henry Irving in the pulp-fiction plays and grand but textually mutilated productions of Shakespeare he mounted at the Lyceum in London.

Her gift was her imagination. On stage it sometimes went walkabout, leading her to fidget or forget her lines.

She made on Shaw, at his first sight of her, 'an impression of waywardness: of not quite fitting into her part and not wanting to'. Her imagination entwined with that of gifted people who painted, photographed or produced her. J. S. Sargent portrayed her as the Lyceum Lady Macbeth raising a crown and about to crown herself. The incident is not in the text and was not in Irving's production. Sargent invented it. The picture is his vision of her.

The decades of Lyceum triumph made Irving in 1895 the first knighted actor. Feeling that Ellen Terry should share the honour, the company called her 'Lady Darling'. I wonder if the fond nickname passed into theatre folklore and was tweaked out a decade later to name Mr and Mrs Darling in J. M. Barrie's masterpiece. Ellen Terry wrote, about 1907, to the Peter Pan of the day, proposing herself for Tinker Bell and asking for her part quickly 'as I am a slow study'.

Shaw sought both Lyceum talents for the Ibsenite–Shavian revolution. Irving, however, was probably too addicted to his near-hypnotic command of the audience, as a talisman of which he had taken his stage surname from that of a pulpit spell-binder and in the image of which, I have conjectured in print and the 1987 biography does now, his business-manager, Bram Stoker, fictionalized him as Dracula. Neither was Ellen Terry won for theatrical revolution. Not wholly against her will, she was in thrall to Irving. Shaw could not enlist her to campaign against the moral claustrophobia of middle-class society, because she had never experienced it.

Shaw wrote a one-act masterpiece, *The Man of Destiny*. The Strange Lady is so exactly tailored for her that it brings the reader close not only to Ellen Terry's voice but to her stage presence, occasional absences of mind included. The play's action is designed to demonstrate to Ellen Terry how, by boldness and intelligence, she could outwit the forcefulness of Napoleon – or Irving. Irving took an option but did not put on the play. Ellen Terry did not act Shaw until, after Irving's death and the death of her second husband, she undertook Lady Cicely

Wayneflete in *Captain Brassbound's Conversion*, a play written for her. At the first rehearsal Shaw witnessed her first meeting with the North American actor cast for an American rôle. She 'put him in her pocket' and made him her third husband. He was as much her junior as she had been her first husband's.

The new biography is overladen with facts. The author has amassed them conscientiously and proffers them with a certain elfin sprightliness. The volume would be less bulky had she jettisoned her redactions of other scholars' works on social and theatrical history and had she devised a stowage plan that avoided repetitions. Chugging under the Dent flag of convenience, the book is manufactured in the USA and written in the US language – not always fastidiously; it includes 'normalcy' and 'the Reverend Dodgson'. Occasionally the discourse runs into ambiguity. When it reports that Ellen Terry hung two photographs of Eleonora Duse 'as self-reproachful icons', the reader must guess which actress the author considers the self who reproached herself. The author seems to have discovered a new secondary sex characteristic when she writes that 'men lacked the breasts and white shoulders women displayed'.

In 1988, when Ellen Terry was sixty years dead, the publishers could have made an attractive commemorative book by removing the illustrations from this biography and reproducing them in bolder and bigger format with more telling captions. Some publisher will, I devoutly wish, re-issue the correspondence between Ellen Terry and Shaw in the excellent 1931 edition by Christopher St John, the transvestite literary name of the woman who was Edith Craig's last lover. Shaw's twenty-nine-page Preface, the work of an expert writer, is a more vivid, comprehensive and analytical account of the European theatre in the second half of the nineteenth century than the 1987 monster heap provides.

Pointing the reader's way towards the letters he is introducing, Shaw ends his Preface with one of the most moving sentences in the corpus of English prose, his tribute to literature, as Dubedat's creed is to painting, and his memorial to Ellen Terry: 'Let those who may complain that it was all on paper remember that only on paper had humanity yet achieved glory, beauty, truth, knowledge, virtue and abiding love.'

The preacher from whom Henry Irving (who was born to the surname Broadribb) took his stage surname was Edward Irving, 1792–1834. Born and educated in Scotland, he became a dazzling preacher in London in the 1820s. In 1830 the London Presbytery convicted him of heresy. He was, or was thought to be, the inspiration of an oecumenical sect calling itself the 'Catholic Apostolic Church' and called by outsiders the 'Irvingites' which, in expectation of a second earthly incarnation of Jesus Christ, rested on its recognition of a second dozen apostles. The Irvingite liturgy was an amalgamation of the rites of Scottish Protestantism, Roman Catholicism and Greek Orthodoxy. The apostles consecrated the sect's bishops, who were called by the Greek title 'angel', and the angels ordained the priests or ministers. In default of intervention by the arrival on earth of Christ for the second time, the sect was destined and intended to cease to exist and to revert to its Orthodox, Catholic and Protestant origins when all the priests ordained by the angels had died.

By asking members of its congregations for a literal tithe (one-tenth of income), the Irvingite sect became rich in Britain and the USA. In London it built two churches, including a neo-Gothic one in Gordon Square, the property, in the 1980s, of London University, which uses it as a chapel for several Christian denominations.

Edward Irving died four years before the birth of the actor who took his surname. I imagine Henry Irving was attracted to the legendary fame of his hold on his congregations or audiences. Perhaps he thought 'Irvingite' a nickname that should be adopted by his fans.

*

My essay on Ellen Terry was published in November 1987.
A reader wrote to the paper offering to play me my 78
rpm record if I should bring it to his area of Britain. My
disablement prevented me from accepting his deeply cour-
teous invitation. Another reader has written to me saying
that the Dual company has resumed the manufacture of
three-speed turntables. And a fellow-writer has with vast
generosity lent me his copy of a 33 rpm record which
bears, dubbed from 78s, the speaking voice of several
historically interesting actors.

On that record (Delta DEL 1202) there are five Ellen
Terry tracks, all, according to the sleeve, recorded in New
York when she was in her sixties. I heard again her 'The
quality of mercy' and heard the other tracks for the first
time.

Perhaps in a manner absorbed from Henry Irving, she
transmits a quality of nightmare in Juliet's charnel-house
dreads in Act IV before she takes the death-counterfeiting
drug. In the track from *The Winter's Tale* Ellen Terry
delivers the lines with which she made her stage début as
the boy Mamilius and it is moving to hear her say 'A sad
tale's best for winter'. On that and several tracks she delivers the lines of all the characters in the scene irrespective
of their sex; indeed, she once delivers the initial stage
direction, which presumably has no sex. I wonder therefore whether the recordings are a spin-off of her learning
by heart entire scenes and delivering them in her lectures
on Shakespeare.

On the record she boldly and tunefully sings as Ophelia
and then, as Laertes, comments on Ophelia's turning hell
itself to favour and to prettiness. In the *Much Ado* track
she again speaks all the parts. Beatrice is so quintessentially her rôle that I was moved to hear her say 'there
was a star danced, and under that was I born' – as well as
astounded that she pronounces 'danced' with a glitteringly
short *a*, like the vowel in 'hat'.

The Great Celtic/Hibernian School

With no more than a grain of truth, though a grain that mythology sprouts on, it is said that an Irishman in danger of drowning is liable to call 'I will drown and nobody shall save me'. English people in earshot, myth continues, politely stop trying to save him because they construe him to have declared himself bent on drowning and resistant to all rescuers.

I encountered the drowning Irishman during an English grammar lesson at school (in England). He was mentioned only *exempli gratia* but he has ever since lodged in my imagination as a spiritual portrait of Oscar Wilde.

Between the end of February and 25 May 1895, it seems when you contemplate the cataclysm, Wilde went down, as drowning people are reputed to do, thrice. He called at his London club, the Albemarle Club, and the porter gave him, in an envelope, the visiting card which the Marquis of Queensberry had left there for him ten days earlier. The card is reproduced in H. Montgomery Hyde's biography of Wilde. The words engraved or printed on it are 'Marquis of Queensberry'. Above that in handwriting is 'For Oscar Wilde posing as a somdomite'. Instead of mentally deleting the interpolated *m* in the first syllable, as he would have truly deleted it had he been proof-correcting, and then forgetting the incident, Wilde read through the error to the intended insult or accusation, which Queensberry, despite the apparently legalistic caution of the veil he draped over it with 'posing', had – in haste, anger, unfamiliarity with the act of writing or distaste for it – rendered a nonsense-word. What, after all, would you do were you indeed to pose as a somdomite?

Wilde received the card as the culmination of several

attempts by Queensberry to fling a gauntlet in his face and thus drive him away from Queensberry's son, Lord Alfred Douglas, with whom Wilde was in love. Wilde instituted the libel action by which British custom and law had replaced duelling. Queensberry was entitled to plead that his seeming libel was in fact justified. The evidence he produced in court made it inevitable that he would be acquitted of libel and that criminal charges would be brought against Wilde. Between the acquittal of Queensberry and the arrival of the police at the Cadogan Hotel to arrest Wilde there was time for Wilde to embark for France, where he would be secure from prosecution. He did not go. He stood trial and the jury failed to agree on a verdict. He stood trial again. His second trial ended, on 25 May, in a 'Guilty' verdict and the sentence on Wilde of two years' imprisonment with hard labour.

The sentence did not cease to cause pain when Wilde had served it. Released after two years, he lived in voluntary, impoverished and sometimes pseudonymous exile in various parts of continental Europe. He was estranged from his two sons, who were respectively nine and eight years old when he was imprisoned. Lest his notoriety shadow their future, they were given another surname. Constance Wilde, his wife, who travelled from Genoa in Italy to visit him in Reading Prison in England so that she might tell him gently of his mother's death, did not see him again after that. She died in Genoa in 1898, of a creeping spinal paralysis, at the age of forty. 'If we had only met once,' Wilde wrote to Carlos Blacker on the subject of her death, 'and kissed each other.' Wilde died in Paris in 1900 when he was forty-six.

The Irishman who drowns because his feeble manipulation of English does not make his desire for rescue explicit to those who hear his cries is by no means a literal portrait. In a society that confused heterosexuality with morality and obedience to the law, Wilde made some of his desires too clear for safety. His fictions *The Picture of Dorian Gray* and *The Portrait of Mr W. H.* were wielded against him in the libel action because they disclose the play of

Wilde's imagination and intellect on the homosexual themes with which half of Wilde's bisexual temperament was in sympathy. Likewise, in *An Ideal Husband* Lord Goring discloses the inevitably homosexual component in narcissism (and in the mythical ancient Greek whose name it commemorates) when, just before contemplating his and his buttonhole's reflection in the mirror, he remarks to his butler, who has prepared the buttonhole for him: 'To love oneself is the beginning of a lifelong romance.'

Lord Goring and Mabel Chiltern (to whom he is, by the end of the play, bound to become an ideal husband) are the two dramatic *personae* of Wilde's creation who most tellingly incarnate not only his own wit but the charm and the generosity of spirit manifest in his letters. Lord Goring is thirty-four but, as he tells his father in an expression borrowed from women, 'I only admit to thirty-two – thirty-one and a half when I have a really good buttonhole.' Wilde gave his age in the libel proceedings as thirty-nine and, without help from a picture which, like Dorian Gray's, could age by proxy or even from a green carnation for a buttonhole, was obliged in the witness box to admit to forty.

His mental arithmetic may have been shaky, though in fact you probably need mental agility if you are to flatter yourself about your age, but Wilde was fully in command of the English language – and, for the matter of that, of the French and the ancient Greek. Had he needed, there were many people to whom he could make requests like the one he wrote from Paris in 1891 to the literary adviser of the English publishing house that was about to issue *Dorian Gray* in volume form: 'Will you also look after my "wills" and "shalls" in proof. I am Celtic in my use of these words, not English.' That may, however, be the boast of an Irishman whose mother was a well-known Irish patriot who published under a name that consisted of the Italian word that means 'hope'. The publishers in whose proofs Wilde's Irish idioms were to be corrected were Ward, Lock. Wilde's letters repeatedly refer to them as 'Ward & Lock'. He quasi-proof-corrected the very name of his publishers, clearly holding that two surnames should not be linked by a mere comma.

The finest biography of Wilde is still that given in the editorial connective passages and the scholarly notes in Rupert Hart-Davis's marvellous 1962 edition of his letters, which is triumphant in its knowledge and sense of the period. Richard Ellmann's 1987 narrative biography is more couth (except in calling Hatchard's bookshop a bookstore) than its predecessors. It is detailed on Wilde's North American tour and provides a more coherent account of Wilde's prison experience than he could in his letters, where he avoided describing kindness to him that broke or grazed regulations. Ellmann and Hart-Davies disagree whether Queensberry was the ninth or the eighth marquis. Both prefer 'marquess' to the spelling he chose for his card.

When Wilde was in it, Reading, as the address on his letters indicates, was a prison. Wilde made it a gaol for the title of his *Ballad*. Ellmann rightly recognizes Coleridge as the poet in whose patterns *The Ballad* is chiefly cast but, although he traces his influence on the plot of *Salome*, does not recognize in the diction of *The Ballad* the presence of Heinrich Heine.

Of the photographs reproduced in the Ellmann volume one that is not familiar from other books about Wilde is most difficult, to the verge of impossibility, to accept. A big, rather plump man in drag stoops towards a severed head that is lying on a platter on the floor. (The head is conveniently photographed from the back, so you cannot guess what kind of mock-up it is.) The caption identifies the picture as 'Wilde in costume as Salome'. As such the photograph was no doubt collected (in Paris) and the Salome has a facial likeness to Wilde. However, Wilde believed his *Salome* to be a dramatic masterpiece. He was mistaken. It took the graphic genius of Aubrey Beardsley, whose illustrations to it depict Wilde's face in a full moon as The Woman in the Moon, to make *Salome* into a masterpiece, and the operatic genius of Richard Strauss to make it into another. With more justification Wilde was proud to have written *Salome* in French as a vehicle, which she accepted, for Sarah Bernhardt. Even had his fantasies inclined him towards drag, which despite Beardsley's joke I doubt, I do not think Wilde would have taken part in a send-up of his play.

Wilde's knowledge of Greek was pursued through his public schooling near Enniskillen, Northern Ireland. Classics, the study of Latin and ancient Greek language and literature, was still the core of the public-school curriculum. Perhaps Wilde's dexterity with paradox began when he had to grasp that in the British educational system a public school was one which was closed to all girls and to any boys whose families could not pay the fees. His Greek in particular waxed, winning him praises and prizes, during his undergraduate career first at Trinity College, Dublin and then at Magdalen College in Oxford, where he was a demy. The word, which, like the paper size, is pronounced 'de-MY', is used in that one college at Oxford to describe the holder of foundation scholarship.

Someone who read Classics had not only to translate from the two ancient languages into English but to render an English political speech or newspaper article or passage from a poem in the prose or the metrical verse of one of the ancient languages in the style of the ancient author most suitable to the subject-matter. The knack needed was that of the parodist or even the forger. Wilde, who was in 1891 to write an essay, *Pen, Pencil and Poison*, that concerned forgery, was so adept at the exercises required of Classics undergraduates that he took a first, both in Honour Moderations, the examination that Oxford Classics undergraduates sit in their fifth term, and in Greats, the final examination whose subjects include philosophy, chiefly of the ancient Greek kind.

The knack of the gifted Classics student is probably what the Oxford Union detected in Wilde when it discerned plagiary in his first volume of English verse. It was, however, with entire originality that, as a writer of stories and, above all, of plays for the London theatre, Wilde devised a new English form for the epigram, which is in

Greek simply an inscription or a poem short enough to be one, usually cast in the elegiac metre (in the Greek sense), and for the aphorism, which in Greek is simply a definition.

On his deathbed, mute but not quite unconscious, Wilde was conditionally baptized by a Roman Catholic priest. Conditional baptism is usually administered to adults who seek reception into the Catholic church in case there has been a previous baptism – whose form, however, may not have been valid in Catholic terms. According to Ellmann the precaution was not needed. Wilde was baptized as an infant by an Anglican clerical uncle but when he was four or five years old he and his elder brother were, at their mother's request, baptized again, this time by a Roman Catholic priest. Ellmann associates Wilde's experience as a little boy with the quest of both Jack and Algernon in *The Importance of Being Earnest* for Anglican adult (and possibly second) baptism. The Wilde children's double baptism into conflicting versions of the Christian faith was probably the surest method Speranza could think of to bring up her sons to be thoroughly Irish.

Despite his manful intellectual struggles to perceive Jesus Christ as the supreme exemplar of self-sacrifice, Wilde was, I think, more impressed by Socrates as he is reported or fictionalized in dialogues by Plato. In *The Decay of Lying*, where he used his sons' first names as the names of the speakers, Wilde tried to mould the Platonic dialogue into a narrative-discursive English form, halfway between story and play.

Wilde's remaining in London to stand criminal prosecution is explicable only, I think, by the fact that Socrates was tried on criminal charges of importing new deities and intellectually corrupting young men. He was found guilty by a jury of his fellow-Athenians and condemned to death. Although it would have been easy for him to flee across the border, he put forward the argument, which needs neither faith nor theology to explain it, that if you live in a democracy and have not persuaded your fellow-citizens to change the laws, then you are morally obliged to obey them. So he remained in Athens and in prison and drank the lethal poison that was provided so that he should be his own executioner.

Wilde and Bernard Shaw, the two greatest late-nineteenth-century (and, in Shaw's case, early-twentieth-century) writers of English, were born within two years of each other in Dublin. Wilde's father, a noted and knighted eye and ear surgeon, operated on Shaw's father to correct his squint, over-corrected and left the patient with a squint in the other direction. (Shaw gives a brief account. Ellmann, who seems ill-read in Shaw, ignores it.) In London, where both men were all-purpose critics and playwrights, they constituted what they called the 'great Celtic school' and gave their London plays alternate opus numbers like musical compositions. In his inscription to Shaw in the copy he gave him of opus 1, *Lady Windermere's Fan*, Wilde called the school 'Hibernian', a term which, unlike 'Celtic', has an exclusively Irish meaning. The idea of opus numbers probably came from Shaw, who had an acute musical ear and considerable expertise. Yet Wilde had the surer touch in seeking the literary keynote on which to end an act or a whole play.

Wilde ran risks with 'renters', male prostitutes who often exacted money beyond their stipulated fee by blackmail afterwards. Shaw, a socialist economist whose socialism recognized the rights of his fellow-animals of species outside the human, wrote *Widowers' Houses* (his first contribution to the 'school' and therefore its opus 2) about the rents of slum property. Perhaps the school began to disintegrate when the six-foot-three Wilde, whose addiction to food as well as to cigarettes glints through *The Importance*, became too portly to be able to wear with dignity the knee-breeches he had once adopted as aesthetic clothes for men but noticed that the six-foot Shaw remained bone-thin in his Jaeger suits.

In *The Importance* Wilde created a work of art as vigorous and nearly as moving in its symmetry as Mozart's *Così Fan Tutte*. Shaw's sole gross critical blunder was not to perceive that its seriousness and beauty lay in its design.

During his post-prison exile Wilde's concern with prison reform and the introduction of compassion to the penal system made him a socialist on almost the municipal Shavian pattern. After his death Shaw recognized an un-austere saintliness in Wilde's generosity, which was the equal of Shaw's own.

That strange play, *Saint Joan*, which, when it was pro-duced in 1924, was acclaimed as Shaw's greatest and which is nearly his worst, expresses some of Shaw's thoughts about Wilde after his death. Perhaps Shaw's imagination or his audience's could realize the 1420s only as Pre-Raphaelite tableaux. It is the Epilogue that makes *Saint Joan* moving. Joan, condemned by as scrupulous a court as Wilde was, is accorded immortality by the church that condemned her six centuries earlier. There is a little in her canonization and her admirers' refusal to wish her resur-rected of Shaw's recognition of Wilde as an incomparably great and incomparably tiresome writer.

Yet it was in 1906 in *The Doctor's Dilemma* that Shaw accepted Wilde's tiresome aesthetic faith. At the same time, making his dramatic points, as Wilde congratulated him on doing in opus 2, out of 'the mere facts of life', he laments the death of consumption in 1898, when he was twenty-eight, of Wilde's illustrator, friend and caricaturist, Aubrey Beardsley, who becomes the dying consumptive painter, Louis Dubedat. Before he dies, Dubedat pro-nounces the creed that both Beardsley and Wilde really did believe in, the final two mellifluous and moving clauses in which are Shaw's acceptance of the sanctity of aes-theticism: 'I believe in Michael Angelo, Velasquez and Rembrandt: in the might of design, the mystery of color, the redemption of all things by Beauty everlasting and the message of Art that has made these hands blessed. Amen. Amen.'

Why, When and Where

Collections

Writers who assemble their essays into volumes that are published are sometimes accused of arrogance. It is, however, more arrogant – and much less practical – to expect a reader who lives in, say, Scotland to heed your interesting and amusing thesis if its first and only appearance was in a New York magazine or a multilingual compilation published in Holland.

My first volume of essays was published by Cape in Britain and by Holt, Rinehart & Winston in the USA in 1966. Its title is *Don't Never Forget*. That is part of an inscription Mozart wrote more or less in the English language in a friend's album: 'Don't never forget your true and faithfull friend.'

His spelling of the English word 'friend' was better than Jane Austen's.

The title-essay in the volume explains the source of the quotation and makes it implicitly clear why I affixed it to the whole volume. I consider it vital that human beings never should forget Mozart.

By the 1980s both the British and the US edition of *Don't Never Forget* had gone out of print. Several of the essays, however, are in print, and more are due to be, in anthologies published in the USA.

For *Reads* I have myself rescued a few of the essays that

were included in *Don't Never Forget*. I have variously curtailed and expanded them. In such matters of practical information as postal addresses I have brought them up to date.

In 1987 my second collected volume of essays, *Baroque-
'n'-Roll*, was published by Hamish Hamilton in Britain
and under the imprint of David and Charles in the USA.
The essays included are for the most part fairly recent
work, first published, in several instances, in the USA.

The title-essay, however, is new work, written for the
volume and not previously published anywhere else.

Reads

Unlike my two earlier collections, *Reads* does not contain a
title-essay that shares its title with the volume as a whole.

The essays in *Reads*, unlike those in my two previous
volumes of essays, do not carry a note above the text
about when and where each essay first appeared. I have
thought it more convenient to my readers to stow such
bibliographical information here, at the back.

Should you want to discover the date and original
publication-place of an essay, whether the additions that
expand it are new and whether the essay was wholly or
partly included in *Don't Never Forget*, seek here. The notes
on the essays appear in the order the essays take in the
volume.

Notes on Essays in Reads

'The Menace of Nature' appeared in the *New Statesman*
in 1965 and in my 1966 volume *Don't Never Forget*. I have
made minor amendments to its text for *Reads*.

I reviewed Simenon in the *New Statesman* in 1964 and
my essay was collected in *Don't Never Forget*.

'A Literary Person's Guide to Opera', which I have expanded for *Reads*, was published in *Opera* magazine in
1965 and included in my first collection.

'Call Me Madame Colette' appeared in the *New Statesman* in 1963 and in *Don't Never Forget*.

'Slim Prancing Novelist' has been slimmed since its publication in the *London Magazine* in 1962 and in my first collection.

'Genet and Sartre' amalgamates reviews I published in 1964 (and collected in my 1966 volume) in the *London Magazine* and the *New York Herald Tribune Book Week*.

The essay in praise of and regret for the writing of John Horne Burns was published in the *Sunday Times Magazine*, Britain, in 1964. It was included in my volume *Don't Never Forget*, 1966. Horne Burns's first novel was republished in 1988.

The text of 'Antonia' is in the GMP paperback edition of my novel *The Finishing Touch*, 1987, and was published in Britain in *Gay Times*, also in 1987.

'Lisbon: City as Art' was first published by a magazine, *Venture*, in the USA. I included the essay in my volume *Don't Never Forget*, 1966.

'Don't Never Forget', the title-essay of the 1966 volume that bears its name, was published in 1965 by the *Sunday Times*. It reviews the English translation of *Mozart, a Documentary Biography* by Otto Erich Deutsch (Adam and Charles Black).

'Miss J. Austen' is a curtailed and reorganized version of something that was, to begin with, a 1964 review in the *New Statesman* and that was included in my 1966 volume *Don't Never Forget*.

It also included, under another title, 'The Box and the Puppets', an expansion of a radio talk I gave in 1965 on the BBC World Service.

'The Rights of Animals', which also appeared in my 1966 volume, was published by the *Sunday Times* in 1965. For *Reads* I have, wherever I can, brought the names and addresses of organizations up to date (1988) and have added two explanatory and historical follow-on sections that have not been published before.

The Fabritius painting of a goldfinch is in the Mauritshuis at The Hague. I decided to write about it when I was asked to contribute to a book on the Mauritshuis published, largely in Dutch, in 1988.

The essay here named 'Felines' is a review of A. N. Wilson's novel *Stray*, 1987, Walker. I reviewed it in that year for the *Literary Review*, London.

Also in 1987 and also in the *Literary Review* I reviewed John Heath-Stubbs's volume of poems, *Cats' Parnassus*, Hearing Eye. I have given both reviews titles that include the word 'feline' probably because Auberon Waugh, editor of the *Literary Review*, has privately designated me the paper's feline correspondent.

'Sentimentality and Louisa M. Alcott' was included in my 1966 volume after publication in 1964 in the *Sunday Times Magazine* and the *New York Times* Book Review.

My essay on Ellen Terry, reviewing a biography of her by Nina Auerbach, appeared in the *Times Literary Supplement*, London, for 6–12 November 1987. For *Reads* I have added two follow-on passages, the second of which recounts information and help I have been given and am grateful for.

My essay about Oscar Wilde was commissioned in 1988 by Ben Sonnenberg for the New York magazine *Grand Street* and included in a volume *Performance and Reality*, Rutgers U.P., 1989.

On 1 February 1988 the British non-tabloid newspaper *The Independent* carried a full-page advertisement expressing alarm about Clause 28 in the Local Government Bill which was then proceeding through Parliament. The Clause forebade local authorities to promote homosexuality or to teach its acceptability as a 'pretended family relationship'. It did not define what it was outlawing.

The signatories of the advertisement, who were many and of different political views and whose names were closely packed on the printed page, included (in addition to Michael Levey and me) the Marquess (thus spelt in 1988) of Queensberry.